"... recommend to my readers who are caregivers of chronically ill and permanently disabled spouses... provides insight into the life of a well spouse and his/her loved one... Reading the true life stories... is like attending a support group meeting... a practical book for caregivers of a parent or other family member. I wish it had been available when I was caring for my brain-injured son."

—Diane Rodecker, Newspaper columnist,
THE ORANGE COUNTY REGISTER, "The Challenger" Column

"... brutally honest account of the lives of nine family caregivers... doors are blown wide open... They reveal their innermost thoughts and the most intimate details of their lives... noncaregivers will gain a deeper appreciation... that chronic illness affects the entire family."

—Suzanne Geffen Mintz, President/Co-Founder,
NATIONAL FAMILY CAREGIVERS ASSOCIATION

"... honest depiction of caregivers' lives is a real contribution... the circumstances he describes have broad applications to other chronic disease and disability situations... patients, caregivers and the professionals who work with them, will gain understanding from the insights and information this sensitive and truthful book offers."

—Lilly Cohen, Co-President, WELL SPOUSE FOUNDATION

The Other Victim

How Caregivers Survive a Loved One's Chronic Illness

by Alan Drattell

SLP

SEVEN LOCKS PRESS
Santa Ana, California
Minneapolis, Minnesota
Washington, D.C.

Edited by Paula Becker/Becker & Co.

Book Design by White Light Publishing
Cover Photo © 1996 PhotoDisc, Inc.

Library of Congress Cataloging-in-Publication Data

Drattell, Alan, 1932–

The Other Victim: How Caregivers Survive a Loved One's Chronic Illness / by Alan Drattell

p. cm.

ISBN 0-929765-43-5

1. Caregivers—Case studies. 2. Chronically ill—Care—Psychological aspects. 3. Care of the sick—Psychological aspects. 4. Stress management. I. Title

HQ766.15.H65 1996
363.9'1—dc20 96-7741
CIP

Manufactured in the United States of America

SEVEN LOCKS PRESS
P.O. Box 25689
Santa Ana, CA 92799
(800) 354-5348

For Carole, ever Suzie,

and

for the men, women and children
who are The Other Victims

Acknowledgments

Writing this book was a catharsis for me, and I could not have completed it without the help of a number of people. In particular, I owe a large debt of thanks to the members of my multiple sclerosis support group and to people at the Well Spouse Foundation for their input, encouragement, and friendship. The National Multiple Sclerosis Society, the National Family Caregivers Association and many similar organizations were equally helpful.

Special thanks go to Rosalind C. Kalb, Ph.D., and Mary Lambert, M.S.W., for their expertise and for taking the time to answer all my questions. I also owe a great deal to my wife, Carole, who read my manuscript and gave me her thoughtful ideas and insights.

In the end, I hope this book will provide support and encouragement to people who have a chronically ill loved one. If I accomplish that, I have succeeded.

Alan Drattell
Potomac, Maryland
April 1996

Contents

Foreword

Chronic illness and disability are like thieves. They steal from two victims: the ill person and his or her caregiver. This book is primarily about the other victim, the caregiver whose life is so tightly intertwined with the patient. In most instances this caregiver is the spouse.

My husband has multiple sclerosis. As a well spouse caregiver, I too have experienced the daily stresses, declining quality of life, mental and emotional anguish so movingly described in this volume. I too have had to learn the problem-solving and survival strategies that go with the caregiver's job.

As an active member of the Well Spouse Foundation, a national support and educational network for caregivers, I have shared experiences with many well spouses who care for loved ones with a range of conditions such as Parkinson's disease, heart, stroke, and kidney problems. I have found such sharing amazingly helpful and restorative; and I've discovered that the complex of problems associated with chronic illness and disability is universal. This commonality of experiences also applies to well spouses.

Both partners are confronting significant losses and changes in their lives: loss of strength, capacity, relationships, expectations, security and pleasures. The world may have compassion for the sick partner, but the well partner's altered state of life is not fully appreciated. In every instance the well spouse's challenge is to try to maintain a sense of self, some independence, personal interests, and friends.

Alan Drattell's honest depiction of the caregivers' lives is a real contribution to the growing body of caregiving literature. While the true life stories he tells are about caring for MS patients, the circumstances he describes have broad applications to other chronic disease and disability situations.

I am confident that patients, caregivers, and the professionals who work with them will gain understanding from the insights and information offered by this sensitive and truthful book.

Lilly Cohen, Co-President
WELL SPOUSE FOUNDATION

Preface

When a couple commits to each other, they look forward to a lifetime of love, for better or worse, in sickness and in health.

Yet for millions, chronic illness takes hold, straining relationships and testing togetherness. Multiple sclerosis is one such long-term illness. It changes peoples' lives, causing them to act in ways they never expected. Plans are abandoned. Dreams are put on permanent hold. Life changes dramatically and irreparably. Although one partner has the disease, in truth both suffer from it.

This book focuses on the illness from the caregiver's perspective. Invariably everyone, from health care practitioners to family, friends, and even book authors, is concerned with the sick individual; little thought is given to the person who stays by the side of the chronically ill loved one. We caregivers are expected to be there, to take care of the spouse or significant other. No one seems interested in our thoughts, our needs, or even how we feel. But we suffer too, often silently, alone and anguished. We are "The Other Victims."

In the Beginning...

The diagnosis has been made: your loved one has multiple sclerosis.

There may be reactions of shock, fear, and a feeling of "Why is this happening to us?" Undoubtedly your first question will be, "What is MS anyway?" It is an illness which affects the central nervous system, characterized by inflammation and loss of myelin, a fatty substance that acts as an electrical insulator and protector for nerve fibers in the brain stem, optic nerve and spinal cord.

Because the myelin is destroyed or damaged, the brain cannot transmit its message normally to the spinal cord and from there to the muscles of the body. In effect, the messages are short-circuited, so it becomes difficult to move an arm easily or to control a bladder. The disease is called "multiple" because it is scattered through many areas of the brain and spinal cord. "Sclerosis" refers to hardened tissue in damaged areas of the brain and spinal cord. The clinical definition, however, is only the tip of a very large iceberg. After you have learned the definition, you will want to know how you can deal with a disease which affects you as well as your loved one, a disease which will change both your lives forever.

A number of years ago, distraught over worsening conditions with my wife's illness and distressed at what was happening between us and to me, I decided to join a support group for spouses and other family members of people who have multiple sclerosis. It was heartening to discover I was not alone. There is a virtual army of caregivers out there. According to the Well Spouse Foundation there are as many as seven to nine million well spouses of victims of multiple sclerosis and other diseases. And the National Family Caregivers Association estimates between 18 and 25 million family caregivers in the United States. That is almost equal to the number of people who live in the New York and Los Angeles metropolitan areas combined—about 10 percent of the entire population of the United States.

Eighty percent of all family caregivers are women, and 70 percent are between the ages of 40 and 59. And most of them are on their own: 65 percent of caregivers do not get any help from family or friends, according to the NFCA.

The support group also helped ease my feelings of guilt, anger and despair. The experience of belonging to the group had such a positive impact on my situation I began to think of writing a book about what well spouses and other well family members experience and how we try to cope with a disease which is ravishing our loved ones. Much has been written about those who suffer from MS, yet little is known about how the disease affects those of us who live with them.

I decided to focus the book mainly on the spouses of MS patients. In two instances, however, I consciously diverted from this course, writing about the experiences of Lesley, a lesbian whose significant other has MS, and Edward, a 16-year-old high school student whose mother has the disease. In the chapter on Edward, I also discuss how severe illness in a family affects healthy children.

In most of the stories which follow, I have changed the names of the principal players. I did not change my wife Carole's identity or mine. I've altered the details of some stories to protect peoples' privacy, but readers will still be able to recognize the anguish and anger which permeate the everyday lives of MS caregivers.

The traumas we experience as caregivers to loved ones with multiple sclerosis are the same encountered by caregivers of loved ones with other diseases such as Alzheimer's, Parkinson's, cancer, stroke, dementia, brain damage, chronic fatigue, kidney disease, or spinal cord injury. They have many of the same problems and many of the same frustrations and fears. I want to thank the men and women who freely told me their stories and who confirmed what I have long felt: that we are the other victims of this pernicious illness, multiple sclerosis.

A Brief History

Multiple sclerosis has been identified as a disease for a relatively short time. One of the earliest recorded cases occurred in England. Before he died in 1848, Sir Augustus Frederick d'Este, a grandson of England's King George III and a cousin of Queen Victoria, described a mysterious illness which had affected him for 25 years: recurring symptoms of blurred vision, loss of balance, numbness in his limbs, and paralysis. Although some researchers claim this disease of the central nervous system existed in early times but was not diagnosed, medical records do not back up this theory. Thus, it was left to researchers and physicians in the 19th century to "discover" MS.

Early in the 19th century, physicians confused the illness with Parkinson's disease and even with amyotrophic lateral sclerosis (known today as Lou Gehrig's disease). Some doctors called it "hysteria."

Two European physicians, Jean Cruveilhier in France and Robert Carswell in England, kicked off the age of MS discovery in the 1830s, describing the "new" disease, and in 1849 a German doctor, Friedrich Theodor von Frerichs, diagnosed it for the first time in a living person.

But it was Jean Martin Charcot, a French clinician and teacher distinguished for his work in clinical neurology, who has been called the "inventor of MS." His housekeeper had the disease. The noted clinician listed only three symptoms of the ailment which he had observed in her, and for many years this trio of symptoms led to a limited diagnosis of MS. People who had additional symptoms were thought to have another malady. The first American report of MS came in 1867 when a paper described the symptoms of the late Dr. C. W. Pennock, who had suffered worsening manifestations for more than 24 years. An autopsy showed "spots" on his spinal cord.

Called the most unpredictable of neurological diseases, MS often strikes men and women in their most productive years, between the ages of 15 and 55. Although found worldwide, the disease is more prevalent in the northern temperate zones of North America and Europe and in the southern portions of New Zealand and Australia. It is relatively rare in Africa and Asia, and as of 1992 no cases had been reported among Eskimos.

There are about 350,000 cases of the disease in the United States—some 10,000 are added each year—and about 1.1 million worldwide, according to the National Multiple Sclerosis Society. Sylvia Lawry founded the MS Society in 1946 as the result of a desperate search on her part to find out more about the illness so she could get help for her brother, Bernard. He had been diagnosed with MS, and he was getting worse.

A year earlier, in 1945, Lawry had placed an advertisement in the *New York Times*, which read: "Multiple Sclerosis. Will anyone recovered from it please communicate with patient?" Of course, people don't recover from MS. They live with it in its various forms. Nevertheless, 54 responses came in from individuals as distressed as Lawry. A year later, the Association for the Advancement of Research in MS was chartered. A press release announcing the founding prompted 5,000 letters from around the world, indicating that MS was not as rare as one might have thought. By 1947, the organization was renamed the National Multiple Sclerosis Society.

Today, there are 140 chapters and branches serving people in every state. There are 85 multidisciplinary MS clinics in the United States, and an international movement, founded by Lawry in 1967, links 34 MS societies in other countries.

One of the important functions of the Society is to promote research. In 1945, research on the disease was almost nonexistent. By 1950, Congress created the National Institute of Neurological Disorders and Stroke as part of the National Institutes of Health in Bethesda, Maryland, and in 1995 its research budget which relates directly to MS was $59 million.

What causes MS? No one really knows. Some researchers have suggested a virus may trigger the disease, with the immune system reacting to it many years later. But there has been no substantive proof. Another theory says that somehow the body's own immune system goes awry, turning on itself and attacking its own tissues by mistake. Heredity has also been suggested. But there is no evidence of this either, although a predisposition to development of the disease could be inherited. Dr. Charcot felt strongly there was a hereditary component, but when he interviewed patients with the disease they vigorously denied that anyone in the family had ever been ill with it.

The variable nature and duration of early symptoms hamper early diagnosis. There are eye problems, tingling sensations in the limbs (a "pins and needles" feeling), numbness, weakness of a limb, unsteadiness in walking, giddiness, difficulty with speech, tremors. Later, there may be loss of bladder or bowel control, difficulty swallowing, and paralysis.

The disease is more common among whites than blacks and among women than men (about two to one). Average life expectancy after onset is more than 30 years, and some people survive more than 50 years. Of course, some die within a few years of the onset.

Often, an obituary does not list multiple sclerosis as the cause of death, but it may be a contributing factor. For instance, an MS patient may choke to death because the disease has severely affected the swallowing function. Or, the disease has created instability so an individual falls, hits his head on the ground and dies of the injury.

Although the disease may affect a person mentally, causing personality changes and loss of short-term memory, for example, it is not a mental illness. Neither is it contagious, preventable nor curable, although substantial research is being conducted and drugs have come on the market in the past few years which have provided some hope. As yet, however, no drug has been approved which is a preventive or a cure.

People with MS fall into one of four categories. About 25 percent of those with the disease are **relapsing-remitting**. Here a partial or total remission follows unpredictable exacerbations. An exacerbation is where new symptoms appear or existing ones become more severe. Forty percent of the MS population is **relapsing-progressive**, where unpredictable exacerbations are followed by incomplete recovery, causing an overall decline in physical abilities. The worst cases are the 15 percent called **chronic-progressive**. They have steadily worsening symptoms, with a decrease in abilities which may level off or continue over a long period of time. The rest of the people with MS—about 20 percent—have what is known as **benign MS** which means their symptoms are mild, they may have an exacerbation here or there, but they have complete remission and little, if any, disability over time.

Research on the disease continues. There are studies on myelin, how it is formed and how it changes with MS. There are tissue banks which contain tissues from people with MS to be used in laboratory experiments, diagnostic tests being devised to find MS early in patients, various experiments to gather information about the disease, testing of drugs to help treat those with MS, and studies of immunotherapy to stimulate disease-fighting cells of the body.

Progress is being made in developing ways to help those with the illness. Yet, tragically there is no relief or cure for family caregivers, who often suffer from depression; feelings of isolation; and a sense of being overwhelmed physically, mentally and emotionally by a disease which is strangling them as well as the sick person they love.

Your loved one has just been diagnosed with MS. What do you do? What can you expect? Where do you turn? There is no one solution. Finding the correct path to walk can be as varied as the disease itself. But help is available. The following chapters focus on the stories of individual caregivers. As each narrative raises a unique issue which confronts the caregiver, I will discuss options, tell where you can get information and, in many cases, assistance. Within the context of living with a disease for which there is as yet no cure, I want to provide you with ideas and experiences which I hope will help you improve the quality of your own life and that of your loved one.

The Support Group

My secretary came into my office and closed the door. "May we talk confidentially?" she asked.

"Of course," I replied.

"I haven't slept with my husband for the past year," she said. They had been married for seven years and the marriage was a good one, or so I thought. I knew her husband, and he seemed like a decent man.

"What prompted this?" I asked.

"I don't know," she said. "All I know is that he disappears on weekends, and when he returns home on Sunday night, he tells me he spent the time sitting on a mountain, watching the sun rise and set, and crying."

"Have you been to see a marriage counselor?"

"No, not yet. But we're scheduled to see one next week."

I was leaving that afternoon on vacation, so I told her we'd talk again when I returned. When I got home that night, I related the incident to my wife, Carole, who immediately said, "He's a homosexual." That possibility had never entered my mind, but somehow what she sensed sounded reasonable.

Two weeks later when I returned to work, my secretary came into my office again and confided what she had learned.

"My husband is a homosexual," she disclosed. "He's been having an affair for the past year with a man who's about 15 years older. I don't know what to do. I love him, but I'm really confused. I'm just glad we don't have any children."

"Look," I said, "there must be a support group for spouses of homosexuals. There are support groups for everything these days. Why don't you get a copy of the telephone directory for Northern Virginia where you live and let's check it out?"

She brought a copy of the directory into my office and we scanned the pages until we found such a support group. She took down the number and made the call.

A few minutes later she returned and told me, "I talked to the president of the group, a woman with four children whose husband is gay. She said she knows he still sleeps with other men when he gets a yearning he can't resist, but he always comes back to her. I won't live like that." Later that week, my secretary filed for divorce.

Perhaps if she had attended a couple of support group meetings she might have been able to cope with her situation. The outcome—a divorce—might not have been different, but I am certain she would have been more understanding and perhaps accepting of the situation, for to this day she is bitter about her experience.

Support groups may not be for everyone, but they do play an important role. They are not substitutes, for instance, for a psychologist or professional counselor, but they are important complements. I've seen a psychologist and I also belong to a support group for family members of MS patients. I found out about the support group almost by accident. Someone I knew who had contact with the National Capital Chapter (Washington, D.C.) of the National Multiple Sclerosis Society told me about the support group whose goal was to help family caregivers face the world MS had created for them. In talking with people at the National Multiple Sclerosis Society in New York, I learned that 90 MS chapters report the existence of more than 1,500 self-help groups of all types, including everything from organizations like mine in the National Capital Chapter to family education programs.

Discussions at a support group are confidential. As one member put it, "What is discussed in this room stays in this room." But I can tell you this: the group is a forum for discussing mutual problems and for helping one another cope with situations which most caregivers have been through or will go through. One of the first things I discovered, for instance, is that I was not going nuts. My wife, Carole, often insisted she had told me things; yet I never remembered her telling me. Other caregivers had dealt with similar occurrences, since MS often distorts the memory and comprehension. So I was not crazy. My wife had imagined the conversations; they were as real to her as if they had occurred.

Caregivers experience a great deal of anguish, for they are dealing with a disease which is a living, breathing thing, a parasite which takes over an organism and sends it down a path of physical destruction. You, the caregiver, feel perpetual guilt because your wife, your significant other, your sister, your brother, or your parent has MS—and you are well. Ultimately you also realize you must remain well in order to take care of this person. If something happens to you, the MS patient can be in trouble. Who will take care of him or her, handle the family finances, manage the home, and make the many day-to-day decisions all of us have to make?

Sometimes you wonder why you just don't throw in the towel, get in your car and ride away to a new life. But you can't because you love the person you are caring for. Everyone who comes to the support meetings loves the person he or she is caring for, and we all know deep down that's why we're in the group. If there was no love, you probably would have left, gotten a divorce or just moved out.

One story which made the rounds in our group concerned the man whose wife had MS. He told her he had to go away on a business trip for three weeks and he would have to put her in a nursing home while he was gone so she could be properly cared for. She agreed. The first day she was in the nursing home, she was served with divorce papers. Support group members, for the most part, don't initiate divorce. They stay on. They endure.

The story about the man deserting his wife validates the support group profile, since most of the group members are women. I don't know if there are any figures to substantiate my personal theory that women, who for the most part are more nurturing than men, tend to try to make the most of a bad situation. More women than men get MS; yet more women whose husbands have MS belong to the support group. Perhaps men are more reluctant to expose their feelings in a group setting.

An interesting study done for the National Multiple Sclerosis Society in 1993 showed that people in marriages where one partner has MS tend to remain together. Less than 3 percent of the people with MS in the survey were divorced and less than 2 percent separated. "There can be little doubt about enormous strains created by actual and anticipated physical disability, unemployment and its attendant financial problems," the researchers said. "We could speculate ... that the strains which might ordinarily undermine a marriage often do not occur among MS couples until relatively late in their married life. Since the average age of the onset of MS is about 33 years and since the person may not become disabled for another ten to fifteen years, if he becomes disabled at all, then MS-related disability would not have its effect on people's lives until they are in their mid-to-late forties. By this time, many people will have been married for ten or twenty years, and many will have young children. Spouses who have been married for this length of time, particularly if they have children, may feel such a commitment to each other that divorce is not an acceptable solution, even when MS-related problems have produced enormous strain and conflict."

The caregiver experiences this strain and conflict constantly. In many cases, the MS patient may not be able to walk while the caregiver can. Yet, we caregivers walk with a burden, for we are living our lives for two people. As heavy as our burden may be, we must remember the incredible uncertainty, the stress and the pain the MS patient feels. The disease robs the individual of dignity. My wife Carole has faced each change with tears and foreboding. She cried when we received disabled license plates for our car, and she sobbed when the state took away her driver's license, although by then she had been unable to drive for a year.

I cried too, silently and alone. I encouraged her to look on the bright side each time, but in truth, there wasn't much of a bright side. She knew it and I knew it. Her able-bodied life was slipping away, and there was nothing we could do. I didn't have a magic wand.

Coping on a day-to-day basis is not easy, for me or for the other caregivers. Writing this book has been one way to deal with the destiny which has been handed us. Whenever someone new joins the support group, someone who has recently learned that a relative has MS, he or she has no idea what's down the road. I wish I had known so I could have prepared myself better for my own future. The future, in many cases, is not a bright one, although some MS sufferers show little signs of the disease and some experience extended periods of remission so they can lead relatively normal lives.

It is my wish that this book will provide a road map for "The Other Victims," although the road will still be bumpy. My ray of hope for you is this: as the caregiver, be true to yourself. What is right for one person may not be right for the next. We are all shaped by our experience and nurtured by our values. MS is a leveling experience for the caregiver; it tests our physical and emotional strength. I cannot fault anyone who walks away, nor can I cheer anyone who stays. You do what you have to do, and, perhaps what is more important, you do what you can do.

The people who contributed to this book have many of the same problems I do; yet each one has a different coping strategy. It's like MS. No two people who have the disease have it in the same way, and no two caregivers deal with their adversity identically.

There is a sameness to all our experiences: a deep sense of loss—loss of companionship, intimacy, sharing, and often caring. The disease sorely tests the strength of a relationship. The good news is that support group members help themselves cope and also gain an understanding of the MS patient's experience and how to be a more effective caregiver.

In a support group, no one judges. Each of us is there to listen, to offer counsel and to commiserate with other human beings who face the same adversities. The people you will meet in the pages which follow are (or were) members of my support group. They all agreed to tell their stories with the hope that you, "The Other Victim," will find the support you need in these pages.

Alan

Our lives changed forever that day in early June 1981.

Carole had been having physical problems for years. We hadn't known it then, but the disease, multiple sclerosis, had made its presence felt 13 years earlier when she suddenly lost vision in one eye. The experience was frightening. Our ophthalmologist said it had something to do with the optic nerve and that it would clear up by itself. It did, in about two weeks.

Then, just as mysteriously, the tingling started in her legs and arms. Some days it was particularly bad. Other days it was bearable. The tingling continued off and on for a number of years. Finally, our internist suggested we visit a neurologist. He put Carole through a battery of tests and decided she was suffering from a pinched nerve. Our internist told us he was relieved to hear that diagnosis, since he had suspected MS. Multiple sclerosis was a disease we had heard of but knew little about.

In the spring of 1981 Carole seemed in particularly poor shape. The tingles had intensified. She was feeling sluggish, and she had experienced several falling episodes. Once again she went to see the internist. He called in another neurologist who wanted her admitted to the hospital for tests. The decision for her hospital stay was confirmed on a Friday afternoon; she was to be admitted on Monday morning. When I arrived home from work, Carole discussed the plans with me and I called our internist to get more details. He said he suspected one of two things: a brain tumor or MS. Our weekend, needless to say, was unbearably long. I did not tell Carole what the internist had thought, and frankly I was fearful. I didn't get much sleep.

Monday morning we were off to the hospital for a comprehensive round of tests, including a spinal tap, which in those days was one of the definitive tests for MS. Today, an MRI (magnetic resonance imaging) can quickly and more accurately determine if a person has MS. On Tuesday night, the neurologist came into Carole's room to tell us the results. In a brusque manner and with a totally clinical approach, he announced, "You have MS."

We were both shocked. In some way, though, I was relieved that it was not a brain tumor. With this pronouncement, the doctor left. I grabbed him in the hallway. "Did you have to tell my wife that way? She's in there crying now, fearful about what to expect. You have the bedside manner of an elephant," I fumed.

He looked at me as if I had breached some form of medical etiquette by letting him know how I felt and by alluding to his similarity to a pachyderm. But when he realized how angry I was, he mumbled some kind of apology and went back into the room to tell my wife that she would be given a regimen of steroids to lessen some of her symptoms. Sometimes, he announced, the disease can go into remission, and perhaps the steroids would help. While this introduction to MS happened to us in the worst imaginable way, this particular doctor is not necessarily typical. There are some wonderful, caring physicians who are committed to giving their patients the best care possible.

When the doctor left the room that day, we looked at each other and knew that we had to be totally responsible for learning for ourselves what MS is all about. It's most disturbing that no two cases of the disease are the same. Some people, in fact, can have MS and yet lead normal lives with few physical, mental or emotional problems. Others might experience numbness in their extremities, poor coordination, fatigue, tremors, spasticity, bowel and/or bladder problems, slurred speech, unstable walking, partial or complete paralysis, problems with sexual function, problems with short-term memory, judgment or reasoning.

The bottom line is that the course of the disease is unpredictable and it varies widely from one person to another. In Carole's case, the steroids helped initially, but the disease progressed inexorably. She began to have great difficulty with her balance, progressed to a cane, then to a walker, and now to a wheelchair which is supplemented by an Amigo (electric cart) which she uses around the house. It has also affected her bowel and bladder function and, most disturbingly, it has caused mental and emotional problems.

Experts will tell you that the exact cause of MS is unknown and that no one dies of it. What they don't tell you is that the disease is a slow death, robbing a person of independence and dignity and making them, in whole or in part, dependent on others. The effect of the disease on the victim is both dramatic and debilitating. But the disease also dramatically affects the primary caregiver, usually the spouse or another relative.

In truth, I am as much a victim of the disease as Carole is. MS has robbed me of my wife, my friend, my confidante. Even though we are both determined to create the best life we can for ourselves, we will never realize many of our goals and dreams. We are unable to travel together. We cannot enjoy exploring the sensual pleasures of life, or savor the intimate talks which marked our marriage. Now, when we should be sharing the joys of renewal and independence which come after many years of matrimony and raising three children, our lives are defined by MS.

Throughout our marriage, I always took comfort in the feeling that, no matter what, together Carole and I could face the world. But I never counted on MS being part of the equation. Today, I feel lost and alone. I am the other victim.

Many members of our family don't want to deal with the reality of what is happening to Carole. At one point, she complained about me to her sister. Carole insisted that I was uncaring and not concerned about her condition or her physical plight. Her sister called one of my sons and repeated Carole's accusations, adding that perhaps she should have Carole come live with her. My son told his aunt she didn't know what she was talking about, that she had no idea how much his mother had deteriorated physically and mentally and added that I was doing a fantastic job in trying to cope with an untenable and terribly stressful situation. Carole's sister, not quite believing him, came to our home for a short visit. When she left, she praised my efforts and later called my son again to tell him she had no idea how bad things were and that I was indeed making the best of a very trying and sad situation.

Carole's father, although elderly, is in excellent health. He will visit us a couple of times a year, but his stays usually last only a day as he hurries to escape from a painful reality that his daughter is so physically constrained. In fairness to him, he went through his own private hell with Carole's mother who was sick for the last ten years of her life with emphysema, which eventually killed her. Carole could never understand why he would sometimes leave her mother in the afternoon to take a two- or three-hour hiatus. He was, in fact, trying to salvage some portion of his own life.

Our three children, two boys and a girl, are adults and all are married now. Sometimes they seem ambivalent about their mother's condition. They love her, they are concerned, but they don't visit her as often as Carole would like. They do try to call us frequently. Part of their ambivalence, of course, comes from their involvement with their own lives, with their spouses and their children. But I suspect that deep down each one wonders if he or she can inherit the disease. Being with their mother may be a reminder of their own perceived vulnerability. I know they are upset by their mother's helplessness and her negative attitude. Carole once told her psychiatrist that she and I were a mixed marriage: I came from a family which always looked positively at things, while her family viewed everything and everyone negatively. That point of view has been seriously exaggerated by her disease.

I also have to believe the children remember what a wonderful mother Carole used to be. When they were young, she spent a great deal of time with them, counseling them, consoling them when necessary, and encouraging them in everything they did. She would love nothing better at this stage in our lives to visit them frequently, to buy presents for them, and to be active with our grandchildren. The grandchildren display a variety of feelings toward her. Some of their responses may result from a normal child's curiosity about an adult who can't play with them and who has to motor about in an Amigo or be pushed in a wheelchair. But, despite her infirmity, each one of them shows love for her. When Michael was about two-and-a-half years old, for instance, we were having lunch in a restaurant. At the time, Carole was able to get around with a cane and with support from someone who would hold on to her free arm. When she needed to use the ladies' room, Michael promptly propelled her toward the lavatory door, holding on to her arm and carrying her purse over his shoulder, as he had seen me do dozens of times.

As a caregiver, I'm responsible for all the chores and duties Carole and I used to share. I've learned to cook, shop, do the laundry, and clean the house, in addition to working. I'm even responsible for remembering everyone's birthday and anniversary and making sure to send cards and presents. Carole used to do many of these everyday things, but she no longer can. I often feel what many working mothers must feel these days. When I had a full-time job, I would rush home to cook dinner, often do a load of wash or shop for food, and handle a dozen different chores, from meting out Carole's medications to running the dishwasher. To mask my distress, I often joked about scouring the Sunday newspapers to search out the discount grocery coupons, something my father did after he retired. I used to laugh at him for doing this; now I laugh at myself.

Today, I am retired, but I work from home. I still travel on business and sometimes am as busy working for various clients as I was when I was employed five days a week. I'm fortunate because we have someone living with us full time to take care of Carole. The caregiver accompanies her to the doctors she visits routinely, takes her to adult day care two days a week, oversees her medications, bathes and dresses her, gives her physical therapy, and acts as her companion. Hiring the right caregiver has not been an easy task. We have had a virtual army passing through our house, a house that Carole and I no longer feel is our haven, our home. We don't know where anything is any more. I look in one cupboard for a particular pot, and it's somewhere else. So the hunt begins. I always find it, but not where it "belongs."

Except for a couple of the women, I have not felt comfortable entrusting some of the household chores to the aides. We had one who flooded our kitchen after she overloaded the dishwasher with the wrong detergent, and others who nearly broke our washing machine. Each caregiver is a distinct personality who enters your life and lives under your roof. Some have been morose; others have hardly spoken a word to us. And for some, cleanliness was not one of their primary virtues.

Of course, Carole and I have no privacy. I share my bathroom with the current caregiver in residence. I never minded Carole's underwear being draped over the shower stall door or across the towel bar, but strangers' panties and stockings are another thing. Then there's the toothbrushes. Sometimes I'm confused as to whose toothbrush belongs to whom, especially when the brushes are the same brand.

The cost for a full time live-in caregiver through an agency is enormous, approaching $50,000 a year. For a long time I was fortunate that my medical insurance paid most of the bills. When the insurance coverage ran out, I had to hire someone on my own. Now we have a live-in five days a week and I take care of Carole on weekends and holidays. The cost ranges between $15,000 and $20,000 a year, and I pay the employer's share of Social Security and unemployment insurance, deduct her taxes and maintain copious records.

Carole and I stopped having sexual relations several years ago, something I miss a great deal and I strongly suspect she does too. It just got to be too cumbersome, too painful for her physically and difficult for me emotionally. The physical closeness which had once been so important in our marriage has been violated by her disease. But the part of sex I miss so much is the physical and verbal closeness the act itself gave us. There were tenderness and passion, warmth and physical release. Our sex life was satisfying emotionally and physically. It cemented our bonds of love and devotion.

I met for several months with a psychologist to discuss the ordeal of a marriage which is no longer a haven of caring, where a disease has intruded and done what no force I ever imagined could do to an intimacy and a love that has made living for me so special. Even though the loss has been devastating, I had to hang on for Carole and me. I could not walk away and ignore the words we vowed when we were married, "for better or for worse."

At our first meeting, the psychologist asked me a defining question, "What do you want?" It took me four weeks to realize what the answer was: I wanted my life back. How have I arranged to recapture some of that life? To some, I probably have done very little. But to me I've come quite far, given that I am a man who always felt Carole and I shared our whole lives. I did not marry, for instance, to take separate vacations. I intended to enjoy that part of life with my spouse. But I have learned over time that all caregivers need a break, need time to rejuvenate themselves so they can return to their spouses and face with them the disease which has sapped both their lives. This renewal for me takes several forms. As often as I can, I try to spend long weekends in New York, visiting with my son and his two children. My grandchildren in New York and the ones who live close by are the heart of my life. I try to put aside the time to do things with them that I couldn't do with my own children, and I've learned to be more tolerant of their antics than I was when my children were growing up.

When I go away on business, I like to wrap the trip around a weekend so I can spend some renewal time by myself, visiting museums, going to concerts and sporting events, walking in the woods and communing with nature, just relaxing. At one point, I even took a one-week vacation to San Francisco by myself. I missed not being with Carole, but I did enjoy the solitude, the chance to dine leisurely, the visits to scenic sites. I even rode the cable cars.

Several years ago, I moved out of our bedroom into my own room. Since I now sleep in a single bed, when I travel I opt for luxuriating in a king-sized bed. The big bed is fantastic, and I am able to sprawl, spread and turn without fear of falling on the floor.

There was a time when I just wanted to get in my car and drive away, far away, across the country to another place, another life. There was a time I contemplated seriously committing suicide by driving my car into an abutment or careening down a cliff to nothingness. But I guess my inherent love of life and a deep-rooted feeling that somehow taking one's life was an immoral act prevented me from following through with these thoughts.

There was also a time when I was close to having a complete emotional breakdown. That occurred after Carole spent four separate periods within six months in an institution, capped by her trying to commit suicide by taking an overdose of pills. Her psychiatrist had been suggesting for a number of months that I put her into a nursing home. I disagreed, but when she attempted suicide I had all I could take emotionally. At first, I was terribly angry with Carole; then I realized my anger was misplaced; it should have been directed toward her disease, which had driven her to such a desperate measure. I did put her in a home where she received excellent care, and she was helped considerably by a good physical therapy program. Within a few months, she was asking to come home again. I was hesitant, but her doctor assured me that she would be all right. Six months after she entered the nursing home, she came back home. She's been at home since, and although she will never be, physically or emotionally, the person she once was, there has been considerable improvement so that now she can cope with her disease.

One of the bright spots in this dismal scenario is the way our children supported my decision. They were quite aware of the emotional roller coaster I had been on, and, as one of them told me, they didn't want to lose me too. They were also quite attentive to Carole while she was in the home, calling and visiting as often as they could. They attended family counseling sessions to try to understand better what was happening and to cope more effectively with the emotions we were all experiencing.

When I am alone with my thoughts, I remember our life as it was. I know it will never be the same again, no matter how much I pray or wish it to be so. But sometimes these thoughts of the past sustain me through a particularly rough day or moment. I remember the day Carole and I had our first date. It was a Sunday afternoon. She was walking down the street where she lived. It was raining, and she was sheltering herself beneath an umbrella. She had on a mottled pink overcoat and boots, and on her head she wore a kerchief. Allegedly she was walking down the street to go to the corner bakery. In fact, as she admitted later, she was walking down the street in hopes of meeting me coming to her house.

I'll always see Carole walking down that street toward me. I even see her that way today although she uses a wheelchair instead of her legs. MS can never dim the vision of that special Sunday afternoon, and somehow that moment in time sustains me.

Veronica

My husband, Lorenzo, and I have been married for 48 years. We came from Vermont, originally, and about 22 years ago we moved to the Washington, D.C., area. Lorenzo worked for IBM as a systems analyst. When we had been married for only four or five years, the first symptoms of multiple sclerosis just came out of nowhere. Lorenzo would complain that he didn't feel well, that he was weak. We had built a new home, and he was painting the shutters. He'd be fine, talking while he was painting, when suddenly he'd drop the paintbrush because his hand couldn't hold onto it.

We decided to see the doctor about these symptoms. His diagnosis was: "Oh, there's nothing wrong with you. You're healthy and strong."

But the weakness persisted. After we moved to the Washington area, Lorenzo went back to Boston several times, to the Leahy Clinic, but they could find nothing wrong either. He was really weak at times, and had trouble walking. Then the weakness would disappear, sometimes for as long as two years, as if he were going into a remission of sorts. Nothing would disturb him for all that time. Then all of a sudden his leg would bother him again. Still, the doctors at Leahy could find nothing definitively wrong.

About 23 years ago his symptoms became more serious, and we decided to try the Mayo Clinic in Rochester, Minnesota. Again, all they could say was they didn't know what was wrong. Years later when I sent for his medical records, I saw that the Mayo doctors had indicated MS with a question mark, but they had never told either one of us that MS was a possible diagnosis.

In the Washington area, we went to Suburban Hospital a number of times and then to Georgetown University Hospital. They had a team of doctors who would come into Georgetown and take selected cases. Lorenzo was one of the people they looked at. One of the doctors looked in his eye and he said, "You have MS." That was 17 years ago. The doctors wanted to be absolutely sure of their diagnosis so they gave him a grueling heat test. They brought in an electric blanket, turned it up as high as it would go, and found a flotation of the pupil in his left eye. It was just floating. This symptom confirmed the verdict that Lorenzo definitely had MS.

We had two reactions. One was relief because we finally knew what was wrong. Another immediate reaction was to read all we could find about the disease.

One day shortly after receiving the diagnosis, Lorenzo came home from work crying. He was petrified. "Do you know what happened to me today?" he asked. " All of the sudden, for five minutes I was blind. I couldn't see." Whenever he gets upset about something, he cries. He's very emotional. Of course there was nothing I could do. I just looked at him. This sudden blindness happened twice, each time lasting about ten or fifteen minutes.

Lorenzo returned to Georgetown University Hospital to be treated with steroids. Then, finally, I took him to Johns Hopkins Hospital in Baltimore. The doctor there had all the reports from the other hospitals, and he ordered more steroids to be administered in pill form at home. The dosage must have been quite high or perhaps he got too much so soon after he had been to Georgetown. In any event, he became severely bloated. His skin was pulled so tight that you'd think it would burst like a balloon. I was pretty worried. The regime the doctor prescribed was for me to give him increasing dosages each day for a certain period of time. One night, Lorenzo was in particular pain and the bloating seemed to be worse. I telephoned my son, who lived nearby. I said, "You better come over now because I don't think your father is going to make it until morning."

He rushed over. I called the doctor and told him how bad things were. Lorenzo was so bloated, his ankles were over his shoes. The doctor said, "Oh, it can't be that bad."

"I'm telling you he is bad," I shouted into the phone. So the doctor said to bring him into his office and he'd look at him. We took him immediately. We waited in the treatment room, and when the doctor finally came in, he took one look at Lorenzo and said, "God, I didn't know he was *that* bad." The doctor instructed me to wean Lorenzo slowly off the steroids, reducing the dosage each day, until he returned to his normal size.

Lorenzo was still able to walk at that time, but he was wobbly. Sometimes he seemed to be hobbling. He began using a cane, but he started falling a lot. One time, he fell outside his office building, hit his head on the sidewalk and cracked it. At home he was using a walker. One day he was going down the stairs with it. He lost his balance, and I heard him yell, "Wow!" When I looked around, I didn't see him. Then I looked at the bottom of the staircase. He was knocked out and lying in a pool of blood.

I called the woman next door. "Get in here quick," I yelled. "And bring a towel." A bunch of the neighbors heard the racket and came running. One of them called for an ambulance, which arrived shortly, and Lorenzo was rushed to the hospital. He had about 16 stitches to close up his wounds.

It seemed like he went from one crisis to another. Sometimes he'd be standing at the bathroom sink combing his hair, and he'd get stiff as a board and just fall backward. One very hot summer day, Lorenzo was mowing the lawn. Why he did it on such a hot day, I don't know. For some time, we had noticed that heat was affecting him adversely. While he was mowing, his leg twisted. He was literally walking on his ankle.

During all this time, he remained mentally alert, but he was having so many physical problems. He had difficulty writing and even picking up the telephone on his desk at work. IBM worked to accommodate his disabilities. The company changed the toilet so he could use it more easily, first with his walker then with his Amigo. He had a button he could press and the toilet door would open automatically. IBM was very good to him.

Finally, 13 years ago he went into a wheelchair. He had retired on disability about a year earlier. The Amigo had gotten too difficult for him to operate, as the car had a number of years earlier. In fact, for the last few years he was working I was taking him to and from work each day. His physical condition deteriorated rapidly. He lost the use of his arms and legs, and since he's been in the wheelchair he has been unable to feed himself.

We have five children. Two of them, a son and daughter, live near us. They are a lot of help to both of us. My daughter's son also pitches in. Oftentimes, he stays over and takes care of things in the house, helps me as best he can. He's 19, and a very devoted grandson. He loves his grandfather, and I know he loves me too because he certainly goes all out to help me. I guess that's the way he shows his love for me. My daughter comes over quite often, and she has at times given me relief in taking care of Lorenzo. I'm fortunate because I have children whom I totally respect. And my sister, who lives nearby, is also very helpful.

The most beautiful thing is what my neighbors have done to help with feeding Lorenzo. At first, when I had to feed him three meals a day, I felt I couldn't get anything else done. It was so time consuming, and it was as demeaning for me as it was for him. Here is this once big, strong man, more than six feet tall, having to be fed like a baby. I was just whipped by having to feed him and by the stress of the whole situation.

One day, one of my neighbors came over and said she and other neighbors were willing to help with Lorenzo but they didn't know exactly how to approach it. Would I accept the help? Of course I would! She asked me what bothered me the most, and I said feeding him. I'd go shopping, come home, put away the groceries, do the cooking, and then I still had to feed him. So my neighbor set up a schedule, and for the past 10 years the neighbors have been feeding Lorenzo his dinner on a rotating schedule. Each neighbor has an assigned night of the week. There were tears in my eyes when she told what they were going to do for us.

We have had nurses or health care aides for a number of years. The aide comes early in the morning and stays for two hours to get Lorenzo up at 6:30 a.m., get him dressed, feed him breakfast and get him on the bus that takes him to senior day care. He eats lunch at the senior day care center he attends. On the weekends, I feed him and my daughter and grandson help out. I've had many people in the role of nurse or health care aide. We find them through various local agencies. I never wanted anyone living in my home to take care of him.

It took a long time to find the right person to take care of Lorenzo. It was so frustrating. I would wait for the person to come from the agency and she wouldn't appear. I didn't know why. I'd call, and they'd send someone else. There were so many different people tramping through my house that it almost stopped being a private dwelling. Everybody and anybody walk in. We've even had some steal money and food from us. When we found out, we'd let the agency know, and they would reimburse us. But you can't keep everything locked up. Your life can't be under lock and key. After a while there were so many different agency people filing through, I would tell them not to knock, just come on in. And now they do.

Of course, it's costly to have nursing help at home, but Lorenzo gets 100 percent disability from the Veterans Administration as well as a disability pension from IBM. He also gets Social Security. Without the VA money, however, I don't know how we could handle the financial burden. We were able to prove the MS was connected to his Army service during World War II. I had to dig up a lot of doctors' papers to prove that when we were still living in New England he was complaining of weakness. For MS, the VA gives you seven years to put in the paperwork after you get out of service, since it is a disease they cannot detect very readily. Certainly, they had difficulty detecting it 50 years ago. The VA has helped us in many ways. For example, they paid for an electric wheelchair lift that helps Lorenzo move from the house to the back yard.

Having the health care aides has been a blessing because their being there keeps me away from Lorenzo. I used to resent feeding him so much. I had it after all those years of going from crisis to crisis with him and tending to many of his physical needs, and the feeding was one job I just couldn't take. It was the closeness of it, and often having to feed him when I was hungry myself. Some days I was so angry I felt like throwing the food against the wall. At times, I had to take care of his other needs too. At first I catheterized him, but after a while I got the health care assistants to do it. Particularly in the first years of his illness, he would have accidents with his bowels, which is typical of many people with MS. Invariably this would happen at 2:00 or 3:00 a.m., and he would call me to clean him up. After taking care of him all day, then I would be up all night too. Often I just cried with frustration. If I was going to be a day nurse, I could not be a night nurse too. I have to sleep sometime.

When we were still sleeping in the same bed, he'd get spasms and the bed would shake. Finally I told him I couldn't sleep with him anymore, and I went across the hall to another bedroom. But I could still hear him. I picked up my pillow one night and I went to a bedroom downstairs. It was peaceful, and I've slept there for six years now. I had to run away from him.

Lorenzo was never impotent because of the disease, although that's a problem for a lot of men with MS. However, sex has never been very important to me. I'm content without it. While we were still sleeping in the same bed, I was so tired all the time that I wanted him to leave me alone. But he'd keep poking me. When I started sleeping in another room, he became angry because he couldn't poke me anymore. When we did have intercourse, it would take so long. He had difficulty moving his legs, and he was always oohing and ahhing. The pain he had trying to perform, along with my being so tired, made me hate the whole thing. I'd rather go downstairs and watch TV. Finally, about seven years ago he was diagnosed with prostate cancer, and his prostate was removed. Since then he has become the kindest person I've ever known. The operation, which did away forever with his sexual function, changed his personality.

The truth is, I feel I've been cheated out of a lot of the good things in life. I'm almost 69 years old, and I have nothing to look forward to. Sometimes I pray that he will die and I will have at least a couple of years by myself to be at peace, to do the things I want to do when I want to do them.

When Lorenzo was well, we used to go dancing a lot. When we first moved to the Washington area we enjoyed driving around and sightseeing, but then his personality changed and he started to get very nasty. It had to be from the disease. He angrily told me he didn't want to go driving places anymore; he couldn't dance, so that was out too. So we stay home.

Once early in his illness we went to California on vacation. I still had to take many things with me, like rubber sheets for the hotel bed because he was incontinent, his walker and wheelchair, diapers for him. It reminded me of when our children were small and we would visit someone. We were laden with all this paraphernalia. We vacationed at a resort near San Diego, but we couldn't do much more than sit on the beach for a few hours and then go back to the room and sit there. I was so tired.

One day I had gotten him all ready and dressed to go downstairs to the hotel restaurant for dinner when he said he had to go to the bathroom. He was in there a long time. I got concerned and went to look in on him. He had dirtied himself and was trying to clean up. I just wanted to go down to the beach and walk into the waves until the water engulfed me and brought me peace. I resent him. I resent the disease and what it has done to both of us. But what can I do?

I went through a period of time that I did not even want to see Lorenzo. I used to hear him rolling around in his wheelchair in the TV room, and I would cover my ears trying not to listen. But I've gotten over this feeling. It took the health care assistant coming every day and tending to him and setting me free from the daily caregiving to change my feeling. Now, I can go into the room and watch TV with him, sit down and laugh and talk. Of course, there are still days I wake up irritable. I'd rather not see him then. But those days are few.

I think back to times when we were first married, to the plans we made, to what we used to say things would be like in 50 years. Well, 50 years are almost here, but our plans have gone out the window. I used to resent that fact, but now I'm resigned to the way things are. Nothing is going to change.

At one time I thought of putting Lorenzo in a nursing home. He was still working at IBM at the time, and I was almost flat on my face with exhaustion. I said, "Lorenzo, I'll put you in the VA for only about three months so I can rest." He threatened to sign himself out, so I didn't go ahead with it. But truly I didn't have the heart to put him there anyway. His brothers and sisters, all four of them, have told me that he belongs in a nursing home today, but I want to do what I can do.

If something were to happen to me, I don't think my children would put him in a home either. Lorenzo is a very kind person, and his children and grandchildren love him. He used to play ball and have fun with them when he was well. Our granddaughter, who is 18, asked recently, "Grandma, did grandpa ever walk? I've never seen grandpa walking." She was too small to remember him with a cane and walker.

I've missed so many things in our marriage, like Lorenzo's companionship, and the ability to share things together. One of the things I miss most is traveling with him. We used to travel quite a bit. Sometimes he would be dragging because of his illness, but we managed to go anyway. Now even if I want to go to a movie, I don't have him to go with, so I go with a friend or with my sister. I miss going out to dinner with him too. If we're invited to someone's home for dinner, I want to go but then I realize I'll have to feed him and that ruins everything. I get that block. Sometimes one of my children will sit beside him and feed him. When I have company coming to the house, my sister or one of my children will feed him.

His physical rigidity bothers me terribly. His hands are like claws. When we go out in the cold weather, I try to put gloves on his hands, and I lose my patience because it is so difficult, so frustrating. Once, in anger, I ripped the gloves off his hands, and he just looked at me. I'll never forget the look of sadness in his eyes. Before we had the health assistant, I used to have to dress him. It was difficult trying to get his rigid legs in his pants. Putting on his tie was another problem. And then I had to shave him, and comb his hair the way he wants it so he could go to work and look presentable. Then I'd drive him to work. Even when I was sick I had to do it, although I was quite healthy all those years. I did it with hate in my heart, hate for him and hate most of all for the disease, for what it had done to him and to us.

When I go off now to someone's house for a visit or even to visit one of my relatives in another state, I am angry when I have to come home. Sometimes I cry the night before I leave, knowing what I am coming back to.

When we traveled, Lorenzo had trained himself with his catheter, so we didn't have to take a potty seat with us. If he knows he's going on a trip, he'll take his medication which prevents him from urinating too much. One time when we went to the mall, he noticed his pants were getting wet. A male friend who was with us took him into the men's room while I waited outside. He was gone a long time. We normally carried a reserve catheter with us but we hadn't on this occasion. Our friend finally came out with Lorenzo, and he was sweating. He laughed and told me that the catheter had fallen out and he had a job putting it back on again. I didn't have extra pants with me, and Lorenzo had to wear the wet ones home. Now he wears a leg bag for the urine during the day. At night, he has a larger bag. He has trained himself to have his bowel movements in the morning. He has a commode next to his bed so the home health aide gets him out of bed and sits him on it. Then she washes and shaves and preps him while he is on the commode. After so many years, you learn shortcuts!

When I look at Lorenzo now, I have mixed feelings. Some days I go in the TV room where he's sitting and I really feel sorry for him. I say to myself, "Poor guy, he really wasn't a harsh guy. He was really a good husband and a good father." But some days when I'm uptight and he calls, I go in there feeling like I'd like to see him out of there. Some days I feel like saying, "Don't even call me."

A few months ago, I went for a routine mammogram. The results came back saying I had breast cancer. Subsequent tests show the cancer has spread. I think if I wasn't so darn tired I probably wouldn't have gotten this disease. Now what? Lorenzo told one of our friends that he feels really bad because every time he was in the hospital, I was by his side. Now he can't even be with me. He cried.

I don't think I've felt rested any time in the last 20 years. One time my daughter suggested we put Lorenzo in the hospital for physical therapy so I could rest. While he was there, they ran some tests and found he had a large tumor in his stomach. So they operated on it, and the doctor kept him in the hospital a little longer than necessary just to give me a rest. Somehow Lorenzo knew this, and when he got home he said, "You kept me in the hospital just so you could have a rest. Well, you had your rest." I just looked at him. I should have had a longer rest. That's how I felt, deep inside. That's when the hateful feelings start.

I've gone through trying times, times when I was up to my neck in problems and fed up with everything. I would get Lorenzo dressed and push him down the hallway to the TV room so he could watch his favorite program. I would hold that wheelchair coming through the kitchen into the hallway, and I shouldn't say this, but that stairwell looked very tempting. I'd tell myself, "Veronica, snap out of it."

There have been times I wished Lorenzo would die. I felt, "Why doesn't God take him?" You get to that point where you just can't take anymore. If it hadn't been for my neighbors, the home health aides, and the VA, I swear I don't know what I would have done. I wouldn't have survived. No one can truly understand if they haven't been there. No one can ever know how severely MS affects the well spouse.

Six months after Veronica was diagnosed with cancer, she died. The disease had spread throughout her entire body. In the weeks before she died, she told a friend, "It's too bad that I had to get sick to get some rest, to get peace." Today, Lorenzo is being cared for at home by a full-time home health aide hired by his children.

One of the key issues which Veronica's story clearly illustrates is the caregiver's need for help. Veronica's family, neighbors, and friends made a significant effort to assist her. But what about the caregiver who has no family nearby? You must learn to ask for what you need. Barbara Schuyler is a Licensed Clinical Social Worker practicing in Columbia, Maryland. She says, "Realize that it's a strength to ask for help when you need it, not a weakness."

A caregiver recently wrote to Dear Abby with the following plea: "I am the sole caregiver for my husband, who has a devastating illness for which there is no cure. He can't walk, talk, express himself or take care of his personal hygiene. He will not get any better. This is my plea: If you are my friend or acquaintance and you see me at the grocery store or beauty shop, please do not ask me how my husband is.

"I know you care and are concerned, but a kinder way to show it would be to allow me a few minutes of normalcy. Ask me where the macaroni is, brag about your kids or recommend a movie I can rent... So should you see me somewhere, please realize that I'm having a brief reprieve and need some time to not think—or talk—about my husband's illness."

Veronica was typical of the many caregivers who suffer from burnout caused by frustration, stress, and anger directed toward the disease and what it does to them and to their relationships. Help is out there, however, for the many Veronicas in our midst. Many of the following chapters provide information on what's available and how to get it.

Alice

The day before Veronica died, her sister and her daughter told me she had roused from her stupor and blurted out, "Alice, I told you. Make sure you remember. Don't let it happen to you, what happened to me."

Veronica and I were good friends and her death had a tremendous impact on me. We used to go out to lunch and she would tell me about all the times she would have to go to IBM to change Lorenzo when he would have an accident. Those times just tore her up. Lorenzo would sit there and stare at her until she did something for him, like take a crumb off his shirt—things like that. She had built up so much anger inside herself, and she always used to say, "I only hope I have a couple of good years left to myself."

Veronica was always tired. Lorenzo would come in, being wheeled into the room with a big smile. Everyone acted so jovial with him, and yet here was Veronica, dragging and ignored. Whatever she did, she felt, it wasn't right and it wasn't enough. She always asked, "When is it going to be my turn?"

Her death made me think about my life. I asked myself, "What do I really want?" At one time, for instance, I worked because I really wanted to. Now, I'm literally working because I have to, because John's income pays only for his health care and the house expenses. I pay for everything else. But our problem is about much more than money. It's about abuse—verbal abuse—that has been going on since we were married 39 years ago. It's about a marriage that is no longer a marriage. It's about a life that has become one of desperation and living from one crisis to the next. It's about wanting to have a few good years for me. I'm seriously thinking about a separation.

John was diagnosed with MS in December 1970. The doctors did a history and traced his first symptoms back to when he was in graduate school in 1948, right after he got out of the Marines. The first problem was with his eyes. He thought he had a sinus infection because his eye got all blurry. When he went home on Christmas holiday, he went to see an ophthalmologist, who suggested he get a head x-ray and see a neurologist.

Then the blurriness cleared up and he didn't do anything more about it because he had to get back to school. He did have the x-rays taken, but he never went to see the neurologist. He wasn't wearing glasses at that time, and his good eye was able to compensate for the one with blurred vision. Since that time, the vision in his bad eye has always been 20/200, which glasses have been unable to correct.

John and I were married in 1955. Two years later he twisted his right ankle. He favored it after that, but it healed. The following year he twisted it again and hurt it really badly this time, so he had it x-rayed. Apparently there was no break, and he just favored it again and it healed. From then on he had a slight limp, which he attributed to the fact that he was favoring the leg for so long. But the limp got progressively worse.

John was always considered clumsy. He was a chemist and in school, when he did lab work, he always dropped things. He began to have tingling in his extremities, but it didn't seem serious. Then balance became a problem. He would weave and hang onto walls and chairs. I was pushing him to see a doctor again because I thought people at work might think he was drunk. Finally he did see a doctor, and the doctor told us he had MS.

Our children, a boy and two girls, were all quite young at the time. The four of us were sitting in the waiting room at the hospital when the doctor came in. "Your husband has MS, " he said. Then he turned and walked away. That was the last time we ever saw him. We didn't even know what MS was. When John had gone in for the initial appointment, the doctor told him he could have MS, but he also said he could have any one of four different things. I went home and looked them all up in a medical dictionary. When I learned he had MS, I researched the disease more thoroughly, and John researched it as well. He contacted the National Institutes of Health in Bethesda, Maryland, and every hospital imaginable. Because of his discipline as a chemist, he's very thorough in his research.

The verdict just numbed me. I had three children. The oldest was 13, and I was not working because I was home taking care of them. John was working for a chemical company in Cleveland at the time. Right after the company learned about his diagnosis, they called him in on a Friday afternoon and told him what a great job he was doing. On Monday, there was a mass layoff, and he was included. At the time, there was no federal law requiring employers to show cooperation with and consideration for disabled people. So John went to another company in the Cleveland area.

They told him they would love to have him on board but their medical insurance would not allow them to hire him. They suggested he work as a temporary for six months and then maybe the insurance company would change its requirements, especially after seeing he could handle the job. He worked for six months, never missed a day, and at the end of that time they said the insurance company would not authorize hiring him as a regular employee because of the MS.

He had some contacts in the Federal Government, so we decided to move to Maryland to work with a federal agency. That way he could get health insurance and other benefits. Some months after moving to Maryland John contacted some of his former colleagues at the chemical company that had laid him off. He asked them why he had been let go after being told just a few days earlier that he was doing a fantastic job. They told him, unofficially, that he was let go because he had MS; there was no recourse, they added.

Because John had a problem with his balance, he could not use a cane. He would just hold onto walls and furniture and drag his right foot, sort of like a drop foot. He would trip a lot and eventually it got to a point where he seemed drunk. So he reluctantly went for physical therapy, and wound up using a walker.

John has never come to terms with his illness. Every time he has to start using some new equipment, he fights it all the way. It was about five years after the initial diagnosis that he started using the walker. By then he couldn't drive and he tired very easily. Finally, he retired from the government in 1986. He was still using the walker and doing pretty well with it. The next thing he needed was a leg brace that went into his shoe and around his calf to help with his gait. To maintain what he could do, he realized he had to have physical therapy on a steady basis.

John's physical decline has been gradual. He used to walk the length of the upstairs hall in our house every morning in order to come downstairs. Now he can't do that. He's been in a wheelchair since 1990. The disease has also affected his thought processes and his personality. For instance, he can no longer cope with more than one thing at a time. If he's talking about something and you want to change the subject, he can't shift gears.

John has always been difficult to get along with. He was pampered as a child. He was the first one in his family to go to college, and his family treated him like a king. He was spoiled and very arrogant. He believes an education puts you at the right hand of God, and he thinks because he is educated he can get away with anything. He has a Ph.D. Anyone with less than a Ph.D., he believes, is inferior.

When we got married, he was already working. I came from an old traditional background. You went from school to marriage and that was it. I pampered and catered to John just like his family had. I'd prepare his breakfast every morning, and his dinner was waiting for him when he came home at night. I stayed home all day, taking care of our home and the children.

We did have a social life, but it was very limited because John is so antisocial. He's been clinically diagnosed by two psychiatrists as paranoid. The diagnosis was made after we learned he had MS, but I think he has always been paranoid because he is so suspicious and critical of everyone. When he was still working, he would often come home ranting or raving about something or someone. I'd just tell the kids, "Daddy's tired," to explain away his behavior. I took on the peacemaker's role, and my children to this day tell me I permitted his behavior because I made excuses for him and never tried to help him face up to his problems.

Since John was diagnosed with MS, his behavior has gotten much worse, particularly since he retired and I started working. The verbal abuse is horrible. He curses me and swears at me. "You only come from Toledo," he shouts at me, "and who are you?" He came from Cleveland, so he thinks that makes him better. After all Cleveland was at one time the largest city in Ohio, and it's more sophisticated than Toledo!

When John gets excited, he shouts. He doesn't want to hear what you have to say because he can't respond to you. He totally blocks you out. When he does this to me, I can only turn around and walk away. But the animosity and anger build up in me. I'm so frustrated at his anger and verbal abuse. It frustrates him too, because he realizes he's not getting the best of me.

Our children, who are adults today, are tolerant of him and very sympathetic to both of us. They understand how I feel. They all say, "We don't know why you stayed married to him when he acts like that. If you left him, we'd understand. You shouldn't have let him get away with treating you like this all these years."

The home health aides who take care of John have problems with him too. He just fired another one this morning. Yesterday he had someone he wouldn't let come back. The longest anyone ever stayed is about four months. There must have been something wrong with her; she would walk around the house talking to herself and laughing at him. She just ignored him, which only antagonized him. "You're just like my wife," he would tell her. When he'd start blowing up and cursing her, she'd say very calmly, "Your blood pressure. You've got to watch it." John would really like a home health aide who is a friend—an educated, intellectual friend who would take care of him, drive him places, have discussions with him, cook good meals and be pleasant company.

I have not slept with John for a long time. The few times I would lie down with him were just totally frustrating to both of us. He has been impotent for nine years, so for nine years we really have not had intercourse. With the constant verbal abuse, I just didn't want to be near him anymore.

He has asked several of the female aides to fondle his genitals and to perform oral sex on him. I confronted him about it one time. It turned out that one of the women, one of the best ones we had, got another job and had to leave. She recommended someone to take her place. That woman was good too, but she didn't stay very long, and after she left, the first woman called to tell me what had happened. She told me he was constantly asking her to lie down with him, assuring her that he could not penetrate her. He only wanted to be fondled and for her to perform oral sex on him. He told her it was okay, that others had done it, and he was safe.

I tape recorded what she told me. But I still wasn't sure if she was making up stories, so I called another aide who had left. She told me, "Yes, he tried to get me to wash him in the shower, saying that he couldn't do it. He made up all sorts of excuses to be touched. And he wanted me to lie down with him all the time."

When I confronted John and played the tape for him, I was angry. I told him he was opening himself up to a lawsuit. He said they were all a bunch of liars. They misinterpreted what he said. "They don't speak English," he barked. "They don't know what I'm saying to them."

I've put my frustrations and my energy into my work, but there are still times I crave male companionship. I haven't sought it out because I'm afraid. It's not the way I was brought up. Sometimes I'll try to satisfy myself, but it's not the same. I don't do that too frequently. Usually I'm too tired.

His condition finally reached the point that I had to lift each foot for him when he went up the stairs into our house. I knew we were going to need a stair glide. Fortunately, through the Veterans Administration, we were able to get a stair glide at no charge. The VA stepped in to help because we fought the government for assistance. Even though John was diagnosed with MS in 1970, we could prove that the first symptoms of the disease showed up within seven years of his discharge after World War II. If we could prove that, the government told us, the MS would be deemed service-connected. Well, John first noticed the eye problem when he was in graduate school in 1948; fortunately he had saved the head x-rays and that was our proof. We appealed his case to the VA four times, and eventually we won. Now he gets 100 percent disability, and the VA provides everything he needs in terms of treatment, equipment and household help. If we didn't have the VA's help, we'd be in deep financial trouble. The retirement pension from his government job is not much, since he only worked for Uncle Sam for 15 years. And the money I make in my job would not be nearly enough to cover his expenses, let alone allow us to have a roof over our heads and buy food to eat.

While my children were growing up, they thought of their father as disabled. He was also always absorbed in his work. I was the one who was with them most of the time. We would go out to dinner as a family and he would talk with them, but it was always on an intellectual level. My oldest daughter, perhaps as a result of his influence, became an electrical engineer. Another daughter is a computer analyst, and my son is a lawyer.

I know some caregivers feel such despair over their situation that they want to or try to commit suicide. I never tried, even though John has made my life completely miserable. Had he been a nicer person, I would have bent over backwards for him. I would have stayed home and done anything and everything for him, at any cost to myself. But with his attitude, I have realized I have to be self-sufficient. If there was verbal abuse he couldn't control, if he treated everyone that way, I could cope with it. When he's with someone he wants to see or when the children are here or when he visits them, he is a perfect gentleman. Somehow, I could deal better with the verbal abuse that started before his illness. I would ignore it because I felt he was tired, so I would just pacify and humor him.

I have a degree in accounting and also a certificate to teach elementary education. I'm no dummy. But John looks down on me because he thinks all the flunkies who couldn't make it in the sciences took the easy courses. His undergraduate degree is from Case Western Reserve, and his Master's and Ph.D. from the University of Kentucky. He is a snob. He's always been very materialistic, and he's lived better than any of his bosses because he was determined to live on the right side of the tracks.

At first I could look away and not focus on these faults because we were building and nurturing a life together. But with the MS, all of his faults became magnified. I've heard that other MS-affected people experience these changes too. If they were selfish before, the disease somehow magnifies this failing and intensifies it so that their selfishness becomes all-consuming. John's stubbornness is like that. He was always stubborn, but now the stubbornness is overwhelming. When he would fall, for instance, he insisted I pick him up. He would not let me call 911. One time he fell and I couldn't pick him up. He grabbed the phone from me, called the health agency and told them to send someone over to pick him up. It took about three hours for someone to come. The person charged for a four-hour visit, and all it took him was about two-and-a-half minutes to pick up John and get him seated back in his wheelchair.

Now I'm debating what I'm going to do with the rest of my life. Veronica's death has shocked me into realizing that things are not going to get better. I've had to ask myself, "Is this what I want to do for the rest of my life?"

I don't wish John any harm. I wish he'd change, but I know he won't. That's why I'm thinking of other alternatives. I don't wish him dead, but I am thinking of separating. He will have to go to a nursing home or get full-time help and have one of the children keep an eye on him. Of course, that will be most difficult since my son lives 200 miles away and our daughters are both on the West Coast.

Originally, I thought I would buy him out with the inheritance I received after my mother died. I could remain in the house myself and rent out a couple of rooms. We'd split the money we got for the house, and he could move into a nursing home or an apartment of his own. Ideally, I could file for a separation, remain married and stay in the house with him, but not be responsible for him. It wouldn't be much of a change, since I say very little to him now anyway. But I don't think that is a very practical solution.

At one time, I was in love with John. No longer. My feelings for him are absolutely zero. I'm totally drained. As angry as I am with him, my heart goes out to him when I see him struggling and feeling so tortured by his disease. Then I get angry all over again at his verbal abuse. Just this morning he called me a "fucking witch," and I get angry at myself for tolerating it.

He has done so many petty things. For instance, I used to use his computer to write things for him. One day, I was using the computer for something of mine, and he asked me what I was doing. I told him it was something personal. He screamed at me, telling me I could not use his computer for any of my things. I got up, left the room and went out and bought my own computer.

No one in the family can escape John's irrational behavior. When our oldest daughter was planning to marry, we got together to discuss an invitation list for the wedding. He hated our next door neighbors, and he demanded that they not be invited. This particular neighbor had offered my daughter her wedding gown, a beautiful dress, covered with imported lace. My daughter was talking with her father on the phone, and she told him about the neighbor's offer. He started yelling, telling her he forbade her to wear the gown. My daughter told him to stop yelling and hung up. She didn't speak to him for six weeks. My other daughter talked to her long distance for two-and-a-half hours, trying to pacify her. Nothing changed until John's brother was diagnosed with stomach cancer, at which point my daughter broke down and called him.

John complained about everything that had to do with the wedding. He didn't want my friend, who was in the calligraphy business, to do the invitations. He insisted on going to a store and paying $600 for the same thing my friend would have done for $300.

When my younger daughter was married a few years later, she said she wanted a small wedding for the immediate families of the bride and the groom. She asked us to look around our area for a place we liked. John acted like he was the only one who had been asked. He did find a place, but it had steps. I found a place that had a ramp, so it would be easy for him to enter and exit. I said, "Why don't you come for a drive and I'll show you the place I saw?" Well, he got very indignant and insulted that my daughter had asked me to look for a place too. Finally, after some cajoling, he got in the car and I drove him to the restaurant I had selected. He never got out of the car. He took one look and declared, "It's a garbage dump."

When my daughter came home, I took her first to the place he liked. She and her husband-to-be spent an hour going through it. We concluded we would have had to carry him in his wheelchair to the bathroom, as well as up and down the stairs. She decided this was not the right spot for the wedding. The rest of the day she was worried, "How am I going to tell daddy?" But she came home and she sat down and explained to him why the place he liked would be so difficult for him and for us. But he had already called the manager of the restaurant, who told him they would be able to accommodate his needs.

At the wedding, we had to take him an hour earlier so no one would see that a couple of the restaurant's employees had to lift him in his wheelchair into the place and then seat him in a chair on the raised platform for the wedding. They made every effort to accommodate him. After the ceremony, they moved the dinner table up to him so he never had to move from his perch. He appeared to be as "normal as possible."

The night before the wedding, I had a buffet at the house, but John decided to stay in a hotel so he didn't have to see anyone until the ceremony. You see, his family is all dead. And, he resents the fact that I still have family living. I found this out about a year after my daughter's wedding, when he went to California to visit her. She had a three-generation picture we had taken at the wedding sitting on her piano—my mother, me, and her. Every morning when she went into the room, she noticed the picture was face down on the piano. "I can't stand looking at that picture," John told her. "Please leave it face down."

We have a picture taken at my second daughter's wedding of the whole family—the three children, John and me. My daughter gave the picture to John to keep on his dresser. He didn't want it, he told her, because I was in it.

Before I go through with the separation, I know I have to get counseling to relieve me of my feelings of guilt and obligation. That's where I am right now.

Does Counseling Help?

Every once in a while, Alice said, John would "get in his mind that we needed psychological counseling. And every time we would talk with a therapist, John would get angry when he heard any complaints about himself. He would back off, leave the session, and refuse to return."

Despite John's reluctance, psychotherapy can help improve a person's overall health, according to the American Psychological Association. Psychotherapy, says APA, is a collaborative effort between an individual and a psychologist. Couples therapy often works too, but as in everything else, both parties have to enter the sessions with open minds and a willingness to change if need be. Carole and I have been through couples therapy a few times, and one of its benefits is that it helped each of us realize what the other was going through and enabled us to understand why we did or said certain things.

If you want to find a qualified psychotherapist, the Association recommends you ask your medical doctor for a recommendation, check with another health professional, or call your local or state psychological association. Other avenues to pursue include checking with a local university or college department of psychology, contacting your area community mental health center, or inquiring at your church or synagogue. Sometimes, family and friends can recommend someone they like.

If you as a caregiver or your significant other who has MS need a psychotherapist, here are the questions to ask when selecting that person, according to APA:

- Are you licensed, and how many years have you been practicing psychotherapy?
- What experience do you have treating people with my particular types of problems?
- What are your areas of expertise?
- What kinds of treatments do you use, and have they been proven effective for dealing with my kind of problem?
- What are your fees? (Fees are usually based on a 45- to a 50-minute hour.)
- How much therapy would you recommend?
- What types of insurance do you accept?

In Alice's case, her relationship with John had deteriorated to the point where psychotherapy would be of little help. Alice separated from her husband a few months after I interviewed her. At first John moved in with one of his daughters, but after a few weeks, his daughter gave him an ultimatum: get your own apartment or go into a nursing home. His irrational behavior, which began to turn abusive toward her and her husband, was more than she could deal with. And the fact that he could not find a home health aide he liked or could tolerate forced her to make this decision. John is now living in a nursing home.

Jack

My situation is not at all like Alice's. My wife Lynn is completely rational. She's aware of what's going on with her and around her. She's very loving, and she does her best to be as little a burden to me as possible. She's never angry if I go off and she doesn't see me for a whole day. She's happy when I get a temporary teaching job, even though it takes a lot of work for me to prepare for the classes and that means time she doesn't have with me. I've been retired from the Federal Government for about six months, but I still try to do part-time work. Keeping busy outside the house helps me maintain my sanity.

Still, Lynn and I have pleasant dinners at home together. We don't go out anymore. That's impossible, for she's completely housebound, except to keep a doctor's appointment once in a while. She puts as few demands on me as she can possibly manage. I'm lucky that I don't have the situation of being confronted by a constantly demanding, unfeeling person.

We've lived with MS for a long time. For many years, although it slowed Lynn down a bit, it wasn't as destructive and debilitating as it has become in the past few years. Lynn and I have been married for 39 years. Thirty-two years ago she first started showing signs of MS. That was a year after our first son, Gary, was born. When the boy was a year old, Lynn's knee would buckle under her when she tried to carry him. Her doctor couldn't figure out why this was happening. She also had a lack of convergence in her eyes, and the ophthalmologist didn't recognize this as symptomatic of MS.

The convergence reverted to normal in about a month or so. The eye doctor diagnosed the lack of convergence as the result of an inadvertent kick in the eye our son had given her. But the lack of convergence occurred again two years later, and no one had kicked Lynn in the eye this time. As for her knees buckling, the doctor sent us to a neurologist. When the neurologist sent her into the examining room, as she walked down a narrow corridor about 12 feet in front of us, he watched her for a moment and then turned to me and said, "She has MS."

I had heard of MS before, but I didn't quite know what it was. I didn't want Lynn to know about the diagnosis so the doctor, at my request, gave her some rinky-dink answer for her knee problem and did not tell her she had multiple sclerosis.

I did some heavy research into the disease, and I was heartened by the fact that MS is not considered a killer. People don't die of MS, I learned. However, since that revelation so many years ago, I discovered that MS does eventually kill, but by way of other diseases. The favorite one, it seems, is pneumonia. A person with multiple sclerosis gets pneumonia, and because of the MS the patient can't fight off the infection. Another killer is starvation. Some people with MS can't swallow, so they can't eat. I heard of one MS sufferer who was absolutely helpless from the neck down, and he died not directly from MS, but he choked on his food because he couldn't swallow properly. This inability to swallow is an MS-connected dysfunction. So the doctor didn't say he died of MS; he died because of suffocation. The immediate cause of death was he choked, he suffocated. But the fundamental cause of death, nevertheless, was MS.

Over the next 20 years or so, Lynn had exacerbations caused by the MS, but she would recover. For example, she would have difficulty in maintaining her balance, and she'd have occlusion of the visual field so she couldn't see out of one eye. When the eye problem surfaced, she would stop driving. Then when it cleared up, she went behind the wheel again. She also had trouble with her bowels at times. Suddenly, she would be unable to control her bowels, and she would soil herself from head to foot. When this happened, I had to wipe her up as best I could and then put her into the shower to clean every inch of her body.

After each exacerbation, she was left in a weakened state; she'd never come back to the way she was before the exacerbation. It was as if she had taken two steps forward, then the exacerbation would force her back a step, and she would never regain the step she lost. That's one of the mean aspects of MS. You think you can get better, but then you really don't, unlike a cancer patient who either makes some kind of recovery or dies.

MS just lingers. You live with it until you ultimately die, and many people like Lynn suffer through most of their adult lifetime hampered by the disease.

When Lynn finally learned what was really wrong with her, her condition was okay. She wasn't having any exacerbations at the time, and she felt relatively well. She was devastated when she learned she had MS.

She had a friend with the disease, and she had seen her friend suffer and go downhill physically over a number of years. Finally her friend, a woman she had gone to college with, died at the age of 29.

Lynn's internist knew this story too, and at my urging, he didn't tell her what was really wrong with her. I would not tell her either, but the cat was out of the bag when, ironically, I had one of my yearly physicals. When my test results came back, the doctor suspected I had cancer. He felt it was time to tell Lynn the truth about her problem, and unbeknownst to me, he told her. He felt she needed to prepare herself for a possible life without me, and to do this she had to be aware of her own condition so she could make plans to deal with her future. As it turned out, the preliminary diagnosis of cancer was the result of a mixup in the lab. The culture showing the disease was someone else's, not mine. I was as healthy as a horse, and still am.

After Lynn learned she had MS, she went to a clinical psychologist. His response to her, was, "So, what do you want me to do?" Maybe he was a little harsh, but he was really right. He added: "You have a terrible disease and you are going to have to learn how to adjust to it."

We have two children. A second son, Roy, was born after Lynn's diagnosis. We consulted our doctor about Lynn becoming pregnant, and he said it wouldn't harm her or the child. He could see no problem resulting from the MS. Well, he was wrong. I had noticed over the years that anytime Lynn suffered an injury, either accidental or intentional such as some kind of surgery, the event precipitated an MS exacerbation. During the pregnancy and for six months after she gave birth, she felt fine. Then she had an MS attack. She lost control of her bowels, there was weakness in her legs, and she suffered from general fatigue. Physically she was unable to carry on her duties of being a mother. We had to get a mother's helper in to work and take part of the load off Lynn.

As usual, she got over the exacerbation, and life went back almost to normal. Whenever she had an exacerbation, we adjusted to it, we shifted gears. But the worst exacerbation was to come. That occurred just three years ago. Lynn was having trouble walking. By then she was using a walker almost all the time, but she could still walk at a fairly good pace with it. She fell at home and broke her upper left leg. The break was so bad she had to go through a hip replacement type of surgery without her hip actually being replaced. The doctors drove a pin from the upper femur ball and socket for about nine inches down her leg. She healed very well after the surgery, but the trauma ultimately precipitated another MS attack. We were waiting for it. She was totally weakened. She could barely walk. As a result of this exacerbation, she now uses the walker only to go from her bed to the bathroom. She uses the Amigo electric cart to move around the house, and when we have to go to the doctor, she uses a wheelchair. I roll the chair into our van and then lock it into place for the ride.

Our children have always handled Lynn's physical problems very well. We never heard complaints from them. "Mother has this condition" was their only reaction. Lynn couldn't do much, but she really didn't start going downhill until 1980. Up until early 1980, she was still working at a local travel agency, helping to pay the expenses so our boys could go to college. She was able to drive. In fact, today, she still wants to get back into the car and drive, although she stopped driving about three or four years ago. I'd rather she didn't drive, but she'll have to discover for herself what her limitations are. She can still use her one good leg to drive, but her other leg is about 70 percent nonfunctional. Before she broke her leg, she was able to hoist herself up into the van. She tried to do it a few weeks ago, but she didn't have enough strength to make it into the van.

Both of our children are grown now and have families of their own. They live out of town, but they visit when they can. They understand our situation, and they're very concerned about their mother and about me. They've told me this many times. They do what they can to help us, but they have their own lives and their own responsibilities to their wives and their children.

Unlike many MS sufferers, Lynn is continent, although she has a daily battle with her bowel and bladder. The bladder she manages by catheterizing herself. She has a problem with her bowel; it's a spastic bowel which means it's either hyperactive or hypoactive. She struggles with that. She doesn't have accidents any more because there is always somebody around to help her. She had accidents in the hospital when she was recovering from the surgery on her leg, because the nurses are assigned so many patients they can't always run to your side when you summon them. These accidents in the hospital had a terrible effect on Lynn. It was a personal indignity. At home she has a potty by her bedside, so if she needs to get up and urinate or have a bowel movement she does. Now she wears a Serenity pad, which gives her peace of mind. Her bowel actually functions normally until the feces reach the rectum where she suffers a great deal of distress in voiding. I have to give her as many as six or eight enemas a day to help her void without pain.

Lynn and I haven't slept in the same bed for years, but this has nothing to do with her illness. I get up at 5:00 a.m. every day, and I never wanted to disturb her, so we have had separate bedrooms. This has not prevented us from having intercourse over the years. I would just stay with her in her bed for a while, and when we were done I'd move back into my room, which is next door.

We stopped having sex after Lynn broke her leg. Intercourse had been manageable up until then, even with her deteriorating physical condition. Sometimes we would just have oral sex, which was enough to satisfy us both. But for the past three years, we have not been able to do anything. It's just too difficult and painful for her. I haven't done anything for myself. I don't masturbate, and I've never had an affair. I have had ample opportunities if I wanted to promote anything. I belong to a folk dancing club, and for many years I've had to go without Lynn because she couldn't handle the dancing. There are any number of unattached women there, but starting another relationship is just too much trouble. Having an affair is a matter of individual choice. I wouldn't go out of my way to have an affair. That's just me.

Before I retired, when I was working full-time, I had to hire people to take care of Lynn while I was gone. I still have people coming in for eight or nine hours a day. I hire the people myself at a cost of $7.50 an hour. For the most part we have had good caregivers, but it took a while. We found a couple of ladies in the area who are quite capable and very caring. Most important, they are reliable. I went through the usual gamut of nondescript and unqualified people. I got good at firing people. One helper was just simply stupid. When she would give Lynn an enema, she would pinch Lynn's ass, digging her nails into the flesh. Obviously she didn't want to be bothered giving Lynn an enema. So she thought if she dug her fingernails into her ass, Lynn would not ask for an enema. When I heard that, I fired her!

Another caregiver told us she had been a nurse for 41 years. She knew her nursing, but then one morning she complained to Lynn that our house was "a hell hole." Lynn called me at work, and I told her I'd be home shortly. I came home and fired the nurse!

Sometimes I go away for a little rest and relaxation. One lady who works for us has a number of friends who do home health aide work, so I schedule their services to cover me for the time I'll be gone. I was away for five days recently and three ladies covered the schedule for that time. I go away for R&R whenever I feel the need and the opportunity presents itself.

Two years ago, I realized I needed someone to take care of Lynn during the day on weekends. I had been doing weekends myself, and when Monday came around I was always wiped out. I learned that the difference between a spouse or relative taking care of the patient and an aide taking care of the patient is that an aide's day's work is over at some specified hour and she can go home and wipe the whole thing out until the next morning when she comes back to work. If I take care of Lynn over the weekend, it means I'm up with her at seven o'clock for the first bathroom call, and it goes on the whole day until midnight and the last set of enemas.

On the weekend, I have one lady come in eight hours each day, and I can do whatever I want while she's there. The aide does the washing and the cooking. She cooks up a couple of chickens at a time, and sometimes she puts together a quantity of salad, enough to last us a few nights. I set the table, serve the food, and do the dishes when we're done. I also do all the grocery shopping. I have a lady come in once every two weeks to do the heavy cleaning. Two hours and she's finished. I'm 70 years old, and frankly I'm slowing down. What I could do 20 years ago, or even five years ago, I find it harder to do today. I sometimes wonder when I'll ever get a break.

Despite everything, there's still a loving relationship between Lynn and me. We have a marriage. We really do. It has not degenerated into a hate contest like Alice and John. But Lynn and I have both been cheated. We're both trapped. She's very much aware of this and we've discussed it often. I don't feel any real pains or pangs of envy when I see other couples walking together or having dinner in a restaurant together or just enjoying each other's physical companionship. I just feel they're lucky, and they don't know how lucky they are.

Lynn has always dreamed about growing old gracefully, but she has come to realize that the so-called golden years are golden only for those people who are in reasonably good health, people who haven't tasted the end of the candy cane that fell in the sand.

I've thought of putting Lynn in a nursing home, and I've come to a conclusion. As long as she is fully rational and as long as we can manage her situation in the house, I will not put her in a nursing home. What would happen to her if I were to die first? That is a matter I will discuss with my sons.

Managing Bowel and Bladder Problems

Lynn's bowel and bladder problems are typical of most MS patients. As a matter of fact, each person I interviewed told similar stories. The National Institutes of Health in Bethesda, Maryland, recognizes that the inability to control the bowel and bladder is highly stressful, sometimes making patients with MS ashamed to leave home. Ditropan can often help control bladder function. Constipation can be treated with several compounds, such as Metamucil alone or in combination with a stool softener such as Colace or Surfak. Milk of Magnesia, Dulcolax or several other treatments may be prescribed. An enema may be needed to keep the constipation from causing serious damage.

Dr. Catherine W. Britell, writing on the Internet (address http://weber.u.washington.edu/~britell/), says there are a number of ways to approach bladder issues. "It's vitally important to form an alliance with a health care professional who understands the pathophysiology of these problems, knows how to treat them, and maintains sensitivity to (the patient's) emotional needs and lifestyle," she writes.

The best way to treat bowel problems is to avoid them, she says. "The first and simplest thing to do is to manage... food and water intakes optimally. A high-fiber diet is good for everybody. (But) for most people with MS, a little more fiber than usual is going to be necessary to enhance regularity." She recommends 4-6 servings a day of fruits and vegetables; whole-grain bread, cereal and pasta products; and plenty of water. In Lynn's case and for many MS sufferers, malfunctioning bladder and bowels is an overwhelming problem and ordinary methods don't always help.

There are some new medical developments which may aid MS patients in managing bowel and bladder problems. Specialists in neuro-urology believe that control and perhaps even a cure for incontinence may be a realistic goal, in spite of the continuation of symptoms in other areas. Some recent successes have been documented using behavior modification, biofeedback, drugs, and surgery.

There are several products which can help make life easier, such as bedside commodes and even a Power Toilet Aid (PTA) which is easy to store and use when traveling. "Discretion" is a small disposable bag, scented and small enough to fit into a purse. It is used for sanitary disposal of incontinent products away from home. A catalog of similar useful products can be obtained from Home Delivery Incontinent Supplies. Call 1-800-538-1036 for information.

In some cases, such as Lynn's, catheterization can ease the urinary problems. New developments in catheterization for both men and women are currently being tested by the Food and Drug Administration. Progress continues on many fronts. Patients and caregivers have learned that the best approach is to experiment with a variety of options, see for themselves what does and does not work, and then consult with a medical professional to devise a plan of action.

Lesley

I'm gay. It is important for you to know this, although I don't go around advertising it. I assume most people just understand my relationship with Karen, although I am continually surprised when people think we're just good friends or sisters.

Karen and I have been living together since 1982. We both had lovers before, she for three years, and I for four years. Neither of us had ever been married nor been in a long-term heterosexual relationship. I think we have always known we were gay, and preferred to be gay. It's our way of life.

About five years after we started living together, Karen began having some weird symptoms. She had just turned 40. She began having trouble with her memory. And, out of the corner of my eye, I would sometimes notice her head shaking involuntarily. Then I'd look at her and it wouldn't be shaking. She fell down the stairs a couple of times. When she drove, she would constantly hit the curb with the car. And she was having trouble at work.

What with hitting the big 4-0, I thought she was just talking herself into being old. However, it became obvious in early 1988 that something was radically wrong. Karen was an office administrator. She had a responsible job, but suddenly she wasn't able to keep up with it. She actually quit her job early in 1988 so we could move, but we were fortunate because her boss had already sensed that something was wrong. When Social Security contacted him, he said Karen was disabled and could not do her job, so Social Security determined the date of disability from the date she quit her job, and she was able to get a disability pension.

Karen was diagnosed with multiple sclerosis in March 1988. A few months earlier, some friends who hadn't seen us for a year had us over for dinner and said, "What's wrong with Karen?" It was clear to them that something was not right.

Karen and I decided she should see a neurologist. She made the appointment, had some tests, and the verdict came back: she had MS. I had heard of the disease before. A good friend of Karen's had been diagnosed with it several years earlier. But we really didn't know much about the disease, what it was or what it could do. Based on the tests the neurologist ordered for Karen, I went to the library for information and concluded the *best* thing it could be was MS. It could have been a brain tumor or Lou Gehrig's disease.

Karen deteriorated rapidly. By May 1988 she was using a walker, and by the end of the summer she was in a wheelchair. It scared me because she got bad so fast I thought she was going to be dead in a year. She had to resort to the wheelchair because she couldn't stand up. When she used the walker, she really had to lean on it. She just lost the ability to use her legs almost immediately.

Tremors, as she calls them, have been Karen's biggest problem. Every time we went to the neurologist she'd ask him about the tremors, and he would say, "Well, what can you do?" His indifference bothered her the most. Now, she can't use her left arm. She has to pick it up with her right arm. Her left arm used to shake. Now her right arm shakes, along with her head and her whole body. When she shakes, she rattles the wheelchair. The tremors have been frightening to both of us.

In the beginning, I took care of Karen myself. At first, she could still get around some. I would call home from work and if she didn't answer I'd start to worry. So a few minutes later I'd call home again, and if she didn't answer again, I'd go home. We got a medical alert button after I came home a few times and found her on the floor. One time she fell in the shower. The alert was connected by telephone line to a local hospital. But Karen couldn't get into the habit of carrying it, so it was never much help to us.

I'm a chemist by profession, and my boss grew disturbed when I would have to take time off work to take Karen to her doctor. Finally he fired me, claiming I could have scheduled the appointments for a Saturday when I wasn't at work. Unfortunately, Karen's doctor didn't have Saturday hours.

When Karen first got the diagnosis of MS, I was in Seattle on business. She called to tell me and said she'd fallen in the bathroom and the toilet tank had cracked and was leaking. I said, "I can't fly home to fix it." So I had to call back to friends in Virginia where we lived and get them to take care of Karen, the leak, and everything else until I got home.

Because state law recognized Karen as single, we could apply immediately for social services. She told the social worker, "I'm single. I don't have a job, I don't have any medical insurance, and I'm sick." Fairfax County, where we live, has a general relief program, and they paid for her to see the doctor. A social worker followed up with us and told us there was a county program which would provide assistance including 20 hours a week for the services of a home health aide.

When we had an aide, I'd leave Karen in bed in the morning when I left for work. I tried not to deal with her until I came home from work. Then I'd have to make sure she was fed, cleaned up and taken care of.

For a long time, she was not incontinent. She had good bladder control, although we worried about bladder infections. She had always had trouble with constipation, but she still maintained some bowel control. The aide and I would take turns catheterizing her. Technically the aide wasn't supposed to do it because catheterization was considered nursing work, but she did it anyway.

Karen maintained her bladder control until a few years ago when we went on a car trip to Massachusetts and she sat for long periods of time in the car. In retrospect, I guess I should have insisted we make more frequent rest stops, but I didn't and she came down with a raging bladder infection. Since then she has been incontinent.

By November 1993 things got to the point that Karen could no longer be cared for at home, so she went into a nursing facility. I had been telling her for quite a while that it was going to reach the point where she couldn't stay at home and I couldn't take care of her. We were using the aide 32 hours a week, and the county said this was the maximum time they could allow us. Social workers would periodically check up on our situation, and finally they told us, "We're going to have to determine if it's neglect to leave her at home."

The neglect would have been mine; so I really had no choice. Although they never actually said they were going to charge me with neglect, they did determine it would be neglect to leave her in the situation she was in. If they could not justify her situation, they would have withdrawn all their financial support. Then we would have really been in a mess. So I told Karen, "When this happens you're not going to be able to stay by yourself."

Before she went to the nursing home, we had some interesting experiences with the home health aides. The last one we had, I must admit, was vigilant. She checked Karen out, inch by inch. And she decided to stay with Karen until she left for the nursing home; after that she went into another line of work.

I got very upset with the first aide we had. She went away for Christmas and was supposed to be back by a certain day. She didn't show up or call. So I got angry and told the agency I didn't want her back. I had cause to regret my action later, because a parade of really strange people came through our house after the first aide left.

Some of these people considered Fairfax County, Virginia, where we lived, to be the end of the world. They didn't want to make the trip, so we had to make do with those willing to trek out to us. One woman kept telling me about how the CIA had developed AIDS in a lab in New England, and released it on purpose! That was just a sample.

Another woman complained about her feet, although Karen said the woman spent most of her work day in the bathroom. Our cat didn't like one woman, and the woman didn't like the cat. So basically, it was either the aide or the cat. She went. One of the best aides we ever had was a man, but he was coming to Fairfax County for two part-time jobs, and when the other one fell through he had to stop. In addition to the aides, the visiting nurses came often to check up on Karen.

Then there were the out-of-pocket costs for drugs since Medicare, which Karen had at the time, doesn't pay for prescriptions. Once I gave the Giant pharmacy a check for $600, an amount I had difficulty scraping together.

Like all MS patients, Karen did a number of things to help herself. She tried chemotherapy in the hospital one time; it helped with some things and not with others. Her mental processes improved, but physically she was worse. That was the major frustration; every time we'd try something I could see some things get better and some things get worse. There were times when she just couldn't think clearly and couldn't get out the right words. People didn't like talking to her because they couldn't understand her. Today, her thought processes are quite good, but when she gets tired her speech becomes slurred. Karen's neurologist has the attitude that "I'll try anything if I think it's not going to hurt you." He prescribed one drug which helped her tremors, but she had to stop using it because it was damaging her liver.

I have discovered that people don't understand very much about MS and the toll it takes on a couple physically, emotionally, and financially. Karen's family has never contributed anything toward her care; they have never even offered anything. I have medical and financial power of attorney for her. Her mother and sister live down South—her mother in Louisiana and her sister in Georgia. Her father died a few years ago.

Before her family understood the reality of our relationship, they thought I was wonderful. When Karen told them exactly what our relationship was about, they had a problem with it. They had thought I was a wonderful person, but when they found out I was doing things for Karen because I loved her, they couldn't handle it. Now, however, I think her mother has a new appreciation for me because she had to take care of her husband during the last six months of his life when he was bedridden with emphysema. However, I still don't think she understands how two women can be in love with each other the way Karen and I are. Karen's sister is no problem. She has a really great attitude about our relationship.

In early 1990, Karen and I exchanged vows in a church ceremony. We belong to a gay church and exchanging vows between loving couples is a common occurrence. It's not really a wedding, but it's similar. Both Karen and I wear wedding bands.

Actually, it was Karen who insisted we exchange vows; I kept saying we didn't need to. But at some point I realized it was important to her, so we went ahead. I'm still not sure why it was important to her. Perhaps it was as calculating as "we've got to do this so Lesley won't leave me." She had been talking about it for a long time, almost since we first started living together and before she came down with MS.

When we decided to exchange vows, we thought it would be best to tell Karen's family about our relationship. My family already knew. They don't understand, but they don't really care. They like Karen and treat her as part of the family.

Exchanging vows is called a holy union. When we had our ceremony, Karen's sister and one of my three sisters were going to be our witnesses. At the last minute, my sister backed out. Her excuse was that she didn't think I was happy and she didn't think it was the right thing for me. I said to her, "To tell you the truth, I'm not happy about a lot of things, but that doesn't mean there's anything wrong with Karen's and my relationship." I think my sister was getting a lot of resistance from her husband; he had a real problem with the idea of a lesbian marriage.

Since Karen's illness and all the resulting trauma and stress, I have thought at times of walking out. I haven't done it because I care about her. I love her. Having her in a nursing home makes my life a lot easier. However, I do feel bad when I tell her I'm not going to do something she wants to do. For example, I'll go get her on Saturdays, and we'll spend the day out. She'll want to spend the night home with me, and I'll say no. I'm getting used to that, but I'm not used to living by myself. It's very lonely. I miss Karen's presence.

I've not really thought about having a relationship with another woman. I do think about sex since that was one of the first things to go with Karen. Her desire for sex and her ability to have it just vanished. It really upset her when she didn't feel the way she used to feel. Today, I masturbate to satisfy myself, but only rarely. One day I might want another relationship;

at this point, I just can't see it. Yet sometimes I feel that I need something or someone.

Before Karen went into the nursing home, we used to travel a lot. A friend of mine and I took her to Oregon where she was born. We flew out together and did all kinds of things. She's been to places no other wheelchair has ever been. At one point, I bought a van and put a wheelchair lift on it. I got her a wheelchair with a back that reclines and the foot rests that go up. I wish I had done that earlier since it gave us a lot more mobility.

When I look at what's happened to Karen, I feel both of us have been cheated. We had such wonderful plans. When our relationship began, I was still in graduate school, going nights. She was attending computer school. Although she had her bachelor's degree, she wanted computer expertise so she could get a better paying and more interesting job. I made good money, and she made fairly good money. We were going to do things someday. Travel, buy a house with the proverbial white picket fence around it—those were our dreams. We almost bought a house the year she started having the MS symptoms. Now I'm glad we didn't.

About three years ago, when I realized the time would come when Karen could not be cared for at home, I started looking at nursing facilities. When I found one I liked, I took her to see it. When her mother and sister came to visit, I took them as well, and we officially got on the waiting list. It took six months for Karen's name to move up to number one on the list and when it did we moved her in. She's still begging me to bring her home, saying she can stay by herself when I know she really can't.

Although Karen is a sweet person, there have been times she's gotten to me. I've yelled at her when I felt I just couldn't take things anymore, especially when she would cry and cry because she couldn't do something or when she was hurting. Sometimes I just couldn't figure out what was wrong with her. A couple of times she was a lot sicker than I thought. Once she ended up in emergency surgery. It turned out she had a gangrenous gall bladder. The doctor said she must have been in terrible pain, but her complaining didn't sound any different from what she usually said. So I think MS affects your perception of pain too. Of course I felt terrible because I hadn't been able to figure out what was wrong.

Recently, right after she went into the nursing home, she wasn't eating enough so she was losing several pounds a week. Finally they decided to put a tube in her. The change was dramatic. Now she had enough liquid and she was getting enough nourishment. Her temperament shifted and she became very positive, more like her old self. Before that she had been calling me, leaving desperate messages, "You've got to get me out of here." I'd get 20 messages a day, and often I didn't even listen to them.

Medicaid pays for Karen's nursing home care. Her Social Security check goes directly to the home and Medicaid pays the rest. At 46, she is probably the youngest person there. The patient population covers a wide spectrum, including the ones who moan and call for help or the ones that are just sort of sprawled out with their mouths open. There are some who will talk with you. When I first visited Karen, people would say something to me and I would try to answer them. Finally I realized they weren't listening to me anyway; they were just talking. The environment is hard for me to deal with.

All the staff at the nursing home really like Karen. But they're stressed out and can't always give her what she needs. Karen hates it there. I understand that; if I were there, I'd hate it too.

The patients in the home and the care providers don't know about our relationship. Some of them think we're just good friends. Others think we're sisters. I get praise from them for being so nice and for being concerned about Karen. We feel it's wisest not to say anything about our being lovers since we don't know how they might react or how they might treat Karen if they knew.

The deception does concern me, especially when I think about a rather infamous case in Minnesota. Two women had hidden their relationship because they didn't want to offend anyone, and when one of them fell dreadfully ill, the other revealed their relationship so she could care for her. The sick woman's parents cut her lover out of the picture, accusing her of trying to harm their daughter. Because they had never let anyone know about their true relationship, the well person could not prove they had lived together, were lovers, and had been committed to each other.

I don't really know what's ahead for us. Frankly, the way Karen started to go downhill so fast when she first got the disease, I didn't think she would live this long. But she seems fairly stable now, so she could be around a long time. I don't see that we have any choice about her leaving the nursing home or coming back to our home. I told her she'd have to win the lottery, and since we don't play the lottery, it's not going to happen.

Karen doesn't realize the pressure I feel because of her illness. She can't see how difficult it is for me. Nor does she understand how much help she needs and that I can't provide this help and work at the same time. She thinks she'll be OK at home by herself. I told her, "If I leave you in the morning and don't get back for twelve hours, you'll have been sitting there wet and nasty and your skin's going to break down; you're going to get infections. They're taking really good care of you in the nursing home."

Options for Care

Lesley took many of the same steps other caregivers take, going from home care to a nursing home. There is an interim option which works for some, and that is a day care facility.

According to the National Family Caregivers Association (NFCA), more people enter nursing homes because of caregiver burnout than because their own condition is getting worse. But a nursing home is expensive, and for some caregivers dealing with the guilt is difficult, if placing a loved one in a home is seen as an end-of-the-line proposition. In many cases, your doctor will make the decision, recommending that you choose the nursing home as the only remaining option available. Home care and day care, the other options, are not cheap either, but for many people either or both are viable, offering the caregiver relief while simultaneously aiding the patient.

Your state or area agency on aging, as well as public and private organizations, hospitals, nursing homes, senior centers, religious, civic, fraternal or neighborhood groups, are good sources of reference, according to the American Association of Retired Persons (AARP). The National Council on the Aging in Washington, D.C., is also a good resource. The Council can be reached at 202-479-1200.

Montgomery County, Maryland, a suburb of Washington, D.C., offers a handbook on adult care which outlines questions to ask and things to observe before choosing a facility for your loved one. Many state and county agencies publish similar materials. For example, you should evaluate the physical environment. Are there disabled bathrooms, adequate lighting, hand rails? What nursing and social services are offered? What types of individual and group activities are available? What is the experience of the facility's personnel? How nutritious is the food being served? Is transportation available from your home to the facility and back, and what is the cost?

Home health care covers a wide variety of services, from nursing assistance to providing custodial care to preparing meals and even doing some light house cleaning. Resources include your state or area agency on aging, social service agencies, public departments of family services, private home care agencies, the Red Cross, Visiting Nurses Association, public health department, hospital social services, United Way and the Yellow Pages.

You can also hire someone on your own, getting referrals from other caregivers or from friends. Of course you will want to check references and to detail the specific duties of the person you will hire. To help you find a home care service provider or agency, contact the National Association for Home Care, 519 C St., N.E., Stanton Park, Washington, D.C. 20002-5809, and ask for *How to Choose a Home Care Agency: A Consumers Guide*. For a single free copy send a self-addressed stamped envelope to the Association. You can also reach them at 202-547-7424. The Association also publishes the *National Home Care and Hospice Directory* which lists by city and state more than 16,000 home care organizations, more than 1,200 hospices and 2,000 homemaker-home health aides. The cost for this publication is $141 (including handling). Send your check payable to the National Association for Home Care, and address your envelope to Directory, at the address listed above for the Association.

You may want to contact the National Consumers League, 815 15th St., N.W., Suite 928, Washington, D.C. 20005, and request *A Consumer Guide to Home Health Care*. The cost per copy is $4. The League's telephone number is 202-639-8140.

AARP, located at 601 E St., N.W., Washington, D.C. 20049, can provide a copy of *Staying at Home: A Guide to Long-Term Care and Housing*.

The NFCA estimates that the market value of a caregiver's services on an annual basis is $10,556. If you multiply that figure by 18 million caregivers, you are talking about a $190 billion "industry" that few people even know about. The NFCA says that on average home health aides earn about $7.25 an hour. The rate charged consumers by provider agencies is often higher.

A nursing home is the final option. Your major problem may be that your loved one has a disease most nursing homes cannot handle effectively. Multiple sclerosis is one of those illnesses, and the fact that many sufferers are not elderly is another concern.

Debby Allen, a long-term care ombudsman in Cleveland, Ohio, says, "MS patients have different needs than older residents (for instance) with dementia that a nursing home would have trouble handling." Long-term care ombudsmen such as Ms. Allen are usually part of the department of aging or health in every state. (In Michigan, they are part of Citizens for Better Care, which is not a state agency; in the District of Columbia they are with AARP's Legal Counsel for the Elderly). Most will counsel families about long-term care services, help define what is needed, provide information about what is available, and provide information on eligibility for public financial assistance. They also act as "negotiators" or advocates in investigating and resolving complaints made by, or on behalf of, nursing home residents.

"I've had struggles with doctors and aides, about medications, etc.," for MS residents, says Ms. Allen. Many times nursing homes will not accommodate these patients because they are geared mainly to assisting the elderly. For instance, a resident with MS in her early 30s wanted to go to college, located next door to the nursing home. But the home would not help her get there. In another case, a female MS sufferer had tremors which were so severe she could not drink water in the glass she was provided. "She was always thirsty," recalls Allen, adding that the occupational therapist should have seen this and come up with a simple solution: putting a straw in a pitcher of water so the patient could have a drink.

When selecting a nursing home for your loved one, you should visit several in your area so you will have a basis for comparison. In selecting the proper facility, you have to consider a number of factors, according to AARP, including the patient's medical needs and your financial resources. You should also look at the need for rehabilitative therapies, such as physical or occupational therapy; participation in social or religious activities; frequent contact with other mentally alert residents; and proximity to allow frequent visits by friends and family members.

When I put Carole in a nursing home, my daughter and I visited about half a dozen in the area. We got their names from my wife's doctor and from various social service agencies. To our horror, the first facility we visited mixed the Alzheimer patients with everyone else, and the administrator told us, "I don't think we can really handle your wife. We're not experienced with MS."

The home we did select was excellent. The Alzheimer patients were in a separate wing, and the population of the other three wings was determined by the level of ability of the resident to take care of his or her own needs. Also, the physical and occupational therapy was exceptionally good, and Carole was able to improve under their program, so that after six months she asked to return home and her doctor told me that he thought she could do well at home.

After you have chosen a nursing home, make certain that you, another family member, or a friend visit fairly often. It's important that the home's staff know the patient has people interested enough in his or her well-being to be involved in their care. By being there, you can monitor the quality of care, ask questions, and request responses to special needs if necessary. You should also attend some of the facility's functions, if possible, such as holiday gatherings and other festivities.

The average annual cost of nursing home care in 1995 was $37,000, according to AARP. In some parts of the country, the cost is much higher.

When Carole was in a home, I paid $4,000 a month for her care. If she had stayed in the home permanently, I would have had to apply for Medicaid to help cover the costs. Each state has different rules regarding eligibility for this coverage, and you may want to consider consulting a financial adviser or an elder care attorney, who specializes in issues of the aging, as to how your loved one might qualify.

For a more comprehensive discussion of nursing facilities, contact AARP at 601 E St., N.W., Washington, D.C. 20049, and ask for *Nursing Home Life: A Guide for Residents and Families*. AARP's telephone number is 202-434-2277.

Caring for the Caregiver

We have talked about care for your loved one. But what about you?

Caregivers suffer from burnout and need time off and time out. Respite care is available. Some caregivers are able to take time away by asking a family member or friend to take care of the person who is ill. If you cannot do this, some nursing homes will allow you to place a loved one in the facility for short periods of time so you can take a vacation and rejuvenate yourself. In some states, Medicaid offers respite programs. Contact your state Medicaid office for more information and to learn about eligibility requirements. Also, contact your state or area agency on aging for assistance.

In Orange County California, the Caregiver Resource Center offers an annual retreat for caregivers. The retreat provides a hiatus from responsibility as well as teaching techniques to manage stress. Activities include classes in art, theater and music; relaxation training; legal issues workshops, and instruction in body mechanics.

"Having time to yourself is a luxury few caregivers get, but for your mental and physical health, you need to make time to pamper yourself, socialize and have fun," says Claudia Ellano, Resource Center Director.

Family and marriage counselor Edyth Peters says that when she became a caregiver to her husband, her knowledge and experience weren't as helpful as what she gained from the retreat.

"You lose yourself in caregiving; the retreat helped me get back in touch with myself," she says. Information on the retreat is available by calling 1-800-543-8312.

The National Council on the Aging offers *Respite Resource Guide*, which provides information on different types of programs. Send $10 to cover cost, shipping, and handling to the Council at Dept. 5087, Washington, D.C. 20061-5087, and ask for Order #2040.

Edward

I'll be a senior in high school this fall. I plan to go to college, maybe the University of Maryland. I want to be an on-air performer in radio or television. I'm the only one who lives at home with my mother. My father is not around; he abandoned us when I was a baby. I don't have any brothers or sisters. My aunt and my uncle—mom's brother and sister—live near us in the Washington, D.C., area and we have other relatives in Washington state, Texas and Chicago.

My mom was diagnosed with multiple sclerosis in July 1989. Before she was diagnosed, she had a lot of problems with her hands and her knees. Her hands would get numb and would stay numb for a long period of time. Sometimes her knees would be numb too. She was still able to walk, however.

On the morning of my 11th birthday, she was really complaining about how her legs were weak and wobbly. She was having a lot of trouble walking and I said, "Mom, you don't seem so well. Maybe you shouldn't go to work."

She said, "Maybe you're right," and called her office to tell them she wouldn't be in. I suggested that maybe we should go to the doctor. We went, and as soon as we walked through the door into his office, she collapsed on the floor. Her knees just gave way. The doctor sent her to the emergency room immediately. She was fine mentally, but she just couldn't walk and she didn't know why. The emergency room doctors said she needed to be admitted to the hospital, and she ended up staying there for more than three weeks. I stayed at my aunt's house in Chicago during this time. While she was in the hospital, doctors ran a whole battery of tests on her, and their diagnosis was MS. I had never heard of MS before, and I don't think my mother had either.

When I came back from Chicago, my mom was walking and she could do almost everything she used to do before she went into the hospital. She stayed off work for about five months, however. She worked for the U.S. government, and had accumulated a lot of leave, so she was able to take the time off. She went back to work in the beginning of 1990, and she seemed to be doing well. I thought she was on her way to recovery and that we would get back to a normal life. I didn't know much about MS, and for a while she kept the facts away from me. She really didn't want me to know.

Over the next few years, her condition got progressively worse. Today she's completely wheelchair bound. She's beginning to experience the shakes in her hands. Her speech is slurred. She's been incontinent for about two years.

Mom retired on a disability pension from the government in 1991. Because there are just the two of us, we're able to get by on her retirement income; we haven't had to go on welfare.

A typical day for us is kind of difficult. I get her up in the morning. I have to physically get her out of the bed, get her breakfast on the table and make sure she takes her medication since she can no longer handle it herself. A home health aide comes in from the Visiting Nurses for three to four hours every day. Medicare pays for this. She bathes my mother, usually just a sponge bath, and she gets her dressed. Once a week, the aide will put her in the shower. Mom uses a Foley catheter which I empty before I go to school. She wears a diaper, and sometimes she moves her bowels in it. I change her or the home health aide does, whoever is there at the time. I prepare our breakfast, and the aide fixes lunch and a snack. When I come home from school, I fix dinner. I also do the grocery shopping. I have a guardian who pays our bills. He's a close friend that we've known for more than 17 years, and he has power of attorney for both my mom and me.

After dinner, I get mom ready for bed. By that time I'm so exhausted I just don't have the time or energy to study. My grades in school are a C average. I'm really not proud of that, but I'm just too physically worn out to do any better. The principal at my high school knows the situation. So do my counselor and a couple of my teachers. They're understanding when I'm late for school because I have to take care of my mother or because she's sick.

The aide comes on Saturdays and Sundays, but she doesn't come on holidays. Then I have to do everything. At first I was embarrassed when I had to clean up my mother or bathe her. But now it doesn't bother me anymore because I know it has to be done. Sometimes she falls and I have to pick her up. She can't transfer from her bed to the wheelchair so I have to help her. She can't stand up or use her walker at all. Sometimes when she falls I can't get her up, and I have to call 911 for help.

Getting the right kind of care for someone with MS isn't easy. One time mom got sick because her catheter needed changing. Our HMO used to authorize an ambulance to pick her up when this happened, but they wouldn't authorize it this time. So I called 911, and they took us to the local hospital. When we got to the hospital, the Rescue Squad told me I would have to get her down to the urgent care unit the best way I could. I called the HMO, and they told me to refuse service and to push my mother across the street to their office. When we got to the office, they kept us waiting for more than an hour. I got impatient and started yelling at the lady at the reception desk. I made so much noise they finally took care of mom. This has happened more than once.

I have two close friends who know about my mom, but they really don't know the extent to which I have to take care of her. For the most part our relatives don't help me at all. They tell me if I need their help, I should just call them. They've been to our house and seen what I have to do, and I feel they should try harder to help out.

My nearby aunt lives by herself and I think she has thought about moving in with us and taking care of her sister. When she does come by, she criticizes the way I take care of my mother, telling me what I'm doing wrong or how I should do things. I feel angry when she says these things, but I don't let her know I am irritated. I just don't listen to her. She has finally gotten the hint that I'm not listening, so now she'll say, "Well, let me suggest to you…" and I just say, "Okay," and don't pay any attention to her. We do have a lot of friends from my mother's church who help out. They bring us dinner once in a while or just come over to be supportive. I would say our friends have been more of a family to us than our blood relations.

Mom knew there would be a time when I would have to take care of her and of our home, so she prepared me. Right after we learned she had MS, she told me she would show me how to cook, wash clothes, and clean the house. She and I have always been very close, and I've always been very protective of her, even before she was diagnosed with MS. I guess I was always concerned about her safety and about her in general because there was nobody else at home to be concerned.

When you're taking care of someone with MS you need to find ways to help yourself. I belong to a support group for kids that the local chapter of the National MS Society sponsors. I find it helpful to share my experiences and to listen to those of others. I haven't been to a therapist or a psychologist, but I do talk my problems over with a close friend, someone who's like a grandmother to me. She and I have talked about how upsetting it is to see my mother's condition go downhill the way it has. Basically though, I'm not upset nearly as much as I used to be. I finally realized there's no point in being upset because it won't change anything. For instance, I would get upset when I'd see that mom couldn't do things the way she used to. I would feel disappointed and angry with her. But then my friend helped me realize that my anger was not directed toward my mom but rather toward the disease.

People have asked me if I feel I've been cheated out of my childhood. I don't really think so, except in some small ways. Like I can't go over a friend's house and spend the night because there's no one to stay with my mother while I'm gone. Before she was diagnosed with MS, I played in Little League, and even right after she was diagnosed I kept playing because she could still walk and do almost everything normally. But within the last couple of years, I've had to give up a lot of those outside activities.

I do worry constantly that I might come down with MS. I've become sort of a hypochondriac, and every time I get a little ache or pain, I call the doctor to find out what's wrong with me. No matter how many times the doctor tells me that MS is not contagious or hereditary, the question will always be like a billboard across my forehead: Will I get it or will I not get it?

As for the future, I wonder if I'll have to put my mother into a nursing home. I don't want to do it, but it's a possibility I'll have to consider. When I go to college, I'll stay close to home, so maybe we can at least put it off for a while. Mom's mental functioning isn't that good, so I haven't talked to her about a nursing home. I'm afraid of the effect it might have on her if I mentioned it.

During a recent Christmas break, I went to Chicago to stay with my aunt. I left the day after Christmas and returned New Year's Eve because I wanted to spend Christmas and New Year's with my mom. A church member took care of her while I was gone. I really needed to get away. It was great to clear my head and not worry about things for a few days. I didn't even think about mom. I only called her twice—the day I got there and the day before I left.

We had a physical therapist treating her at the time, and later he told me that in the month before I went to Chicago it seemed like she was improving a little bit in her mobility. But during the week I was away, I guess because I didn't call her every day to tell her how I was doing, she began to grieve for me. She went downhill and wouldn't exercise. It was like she was in a state of depression. What the physical therapist told me bothered me for a while, but I can't let myself feel guilty about it.

Talking to my mother in general is kind of difficult. She has short-term memory loss, so I can't talk to her about how I'm doing in school.

Instead I talk to my guardian. My mom asks me about school every now and then, but it's not to give me encouragement because she can't do that anymore.

Her mental state is not good. During the day all she does is watch television. I'm trying to get her into a day care center during the daytime so she will have something to occupy her time and can be around other people who have MS. So far the places I've called say she has to be a senior citizen; she's only 50.

Meanwhile, her condition is getting continually worse. She can't always use a fork or spoon to eat, so sometimes she has to eat out of her hands or out of my hands. She's basically given up because she feels she's never going to get better. She doesn't want to die, but she doesn't try either. She wants people to do everything for her. She's lost the will to fight. It makes me sad, but I have to accept it. I keep asking myself if it's really worth it, going through all the trouble, spending my days and nights taking care of her. But I figure it's something I've got to do, because I love my mom.

How Children Cope

Edward was already eleven years old when his mother was diagnosed with MS. Because he was thrust into the caregiver role, he had no opportunity to go through the progression of understanding the way many children of MS parents do. However, his fear of contracting the disease because his mother has it is common among children of parents with MS. Having regular physical exams and tests will help reassure worried children that they are well. Medical professionals tell us that genetics does play a role in susceptibility to MS; however, the percentage of children who develop the disease when one parent has it is quite small.

The National Multiple Sclerosis Society provides a wealth of helpful information and resources. Many chapters of NMSS have special support groups for children. Some conduct a Family Day to provide support for spouses and children. Contact them at 800-FIGHT-MS, or on the Internet through America Online (Keyword: Health). A more detailed discussion and suggestions for helping children cope with MS is given at the end of Marissa's chapter.

Marissa

My husband Cory has had multiple sclerosis since 1976, but we didn't learn that's what he had until 1980, after he graduated from West Point. Originally, the Army doctors thought his problems were in his head; there couldn't possibly be anything physically wrong with him.

He started losing his sight before we were married, when he was at the Point. He had trouble studying, seeing books and papers, although he was still driving. One day he was driving and I was on the passenger side, and he asked me what color the traffic light was. I realized if he couldn't see the light he shouldn't be driving any longer. That was in 1977.

He graduated from the Point that year, but his sight problem had become so severe that he was given a disability discharge. So he never really served in the active military, and he has never regained his sight. Today, he is considered legally blind. We've tried glasses, and they don't help. He can see things really close up but they are blurred. He cannot read and he only listens to TV.

Cory and I met through a mutual friend when he was still in school at the Point. We started seeing each other, and I became pregnant with our son, Roger, so we decided we should get married. We married in 1979, despite Cory's sight problem. He had no other physical problems at the time, and we were young so we felt we could deal with it. We had never heard of MS. We went to different doctors, some military and some civilian, trying to get a diagnosis. Cory could still walk and function in other ways; sex, for instance, was no problem then.

Before he graduated from the Point, TRW recruited him as a systems analyst. At the time, he couldn't see, but they bought him a visual tech machine which magnifies things about 25 times. Using the visual tech machine meant he could do his job.

We moved to Washington, D.C., and he went into Walter Reed Army Hospital for more tests. At one point he saw several psychiatrists. They were convinced he had a mental problem because they couldn't find anything organically wrong with him—except he couldn't see. Cory was about 22 at the time. We didn't give up on finding out what was wrong with him. After he got out of Walter Reed, we started seeing civilian doctors, and finally we learned at Georgetown University Hospital in 1980 that his problem was MS. By the time he was diagnosed, we had a suspicion ourselves about what was wrong. We had done our own research in medical books and other sources and reached our own conclusion, which the doctors confirmed. Cory stayed at Georgetown for a few weeks. They gave him steroids, which didn't help him.

By the time we received the diagnosis at Georgetown, Cory had more than just a vision problem. He had tingling in his arms and legs. He began to have trouble walking, so he used a cane. For a while, he even walked to work. We found a house only five minutes from his job so he was able to walk. The first cane he used was a blind person's cane, a long white stick. He started using a regular cane when he went to work for TRW. But soon he started stumbling and couldn't use the cane anymore, so I began taking him to work and picking him up.

We were determined to find out what was going on with Cory because we wanted to have another child. I didn't want Roger to be an only child. Of course we were concerned that Cory's problem might be hereditary. We were sort of relieved to finally have our diagnosis of MS confirmed by the doctors, because it meant we could have another child. In 1980 the doctors still could not tell you a whole lot about the disease, or what might happen to the person with it. All they gave us was a little pamphlet, which told us nothing. Today, knowing what I know, there is no way I would have married someone who had MS.

Five years after we got the diagnosis, Cory resigned from TRW. The Veterans Administration got involved, and he was declared 100 percent disabled, so he received a disability pension. By that time he was in a wheelchair. He went from using a cane to using a walker, and then to the wheelchair. For a while he used an Amigo electric cart outside the house, but when he started losing dexterity in his hands he could no longer use that. A few months ago we sold the Amigo to another family where the wife has MS. She's only 24 years old.

Today, Cory is considered to have a very advanced or severe case of MS. I have to do everything for him. He can't dress, bathe or feed himself, or brush his own teeth. He has been wearing an external catheter for the past six years. The health aide we employ empties it in the morning, and I empty it at night.

We don't sleep in the same bed. I've slept in a separate bedroom for the past two or three years. Cory lost his sexual function about six years ago. When he started using catheters, I no longer had any desire to have sex with him. Up until then, we would have intercourse only sporadically. Sometimes we would try and nothing would happen. He couldn't get an erection or, if he did, he couldn't maintain it.

I haven't had any intimate relationships with other men. Sex right now is not a big concern for me. I'm only 36 years old, and I look at things this way: I'm not going to be taking care of Cory all my life. I feel I am still young enough that I will have my own life one day. I don't even masturbate. I just never think about sex. Sometimes my friends talk to me about having sex. But to do that, I would have to feel it was right for me. I would have to be able to live with that decision.

Right now my priority is raising our two sons. After Cory was diagnosed, we had another little boy, Randy. I want to make sure Randy and his older brother, Roger, are raised properly, that they're healthy and that one day they'll be independent and able to be on their own. Then perhaps I can think about having a life. I've brought up the children by myself. Roger was very close to Cory because Cory had time to be with him before he was actually completely disabled. They could still do things together.

On the other hand, Randy has never known Cory like a normal father-son relationship. To Randy, Cory has always been disabled. He doesn't know his father any other way. He's never said, "Gee, I wish my father could come out and play ball with me the way other fathers do with their sons." But when Randy was four years old, I had him start seeing a therapist. I could already see that he was inordinately angry. Of course, a child that young cannot express himself, but I knew there was something wrong and, by God, I was determined to get help for my child.

Today, Randy is a teenager. When he originally started seeing a therapist, I feared he would hurt his father. That's how angry he was. He didn't even want Cory around. He would threaten to roll his father, in his wheelchair, down the hill. He never did that, but it was a real threat and I knew it could happen. He was like an older child jealous of a baby. There were times he would do things to irritate Cory, because he knew his father couldn't do anything about it. He would come up to Cory and say something mean to him. Cory would get angry, and Randy would taunt him, "What are you gonna do about it? You can't even get up."

I sent Randy to private school. At first when I left him at school he would cry because he was anxious about being separated from me. But in the end the private school was the best thing for him.

One time the health aide took Cory to see Randy at school, but Randy acted like he wasn't there; he didn't even acknowledge him until the teacher made him do it. There was no way Randy hadn't seen Cory, because he had pulled up in our big van, and he was rolled into the classroom in his wheelchair. Since those early days, Randy has worked out his problems through therapy. He really enjoys being with his father now. He goes into his father's room to watch TV or to listen to sports together, or to discuss problems with him. He tells Cory about school and asks for his advice about things.

Several years ago, Cory started to have difficulty speaking. Today, it's very difficult to understand what he says, but Roger, Randy and I have learned to translate what he tries to say. Roger, unlike Randy, has never needed a therapist. He has always accepted his father, and today he's a normal teenager doing things like dating and playing sports and preparing to go to college.

I've been seeing a therapist for about 13 years, since just after Randy was born. At that point I suddenly realized, "What am I doing? What have I gotten myself into?" Originally, I wanted to discuss my problems with Cory's disease and get some pastoral counseling because of our marital problems. Things were just so difficult in the beginning, when I first realized what it meant to have MS and when I knew things were going to get more difficult and I would probably be faced with raising two children by myself.

Cory had never been the type of person who could express his emotions. For instance, if we were having an argument, he'd just walk away, which made me even more angry. He wouldn't ever fight back or say something, or if he did, he'd say, "Whatever you want." That's not what I wanted to hear. I never really wanted to divorce him, but I think if things had been different, if he wasn't in the condition he's in, we would probably have been divorced.

At first, Cory actually went with me for counseling, but that didn't last too long. First of all, he didn't feel he needed to be there. Second, he thought if there was a problem, it must be with me. His quitting counseling didn't bother me because I realized I needed counseling for me. There were a lot of things I wasn't getting at home emotionally, things I needed to talk about, including problems in my life dating from my childhood.

Our families don't really understand what we're going through. I think they try to convince themselves that things aren't really all that bad. Of course, they call and say, "I wish I could do more," but just saying it doesn't cut it. Unless they are actually going to come to our house and assist me in some way, they're not really helping me just by saying they are concerned.

Cory's mother, who is in her late 50s, does come up once a year from her home in Texas. She stays for a week with him and does whatever needs to be done. This year was the first time she really talked about how bad his condition is. Basically, she's the type of person who usually sugarcoats things. "It'll get better," she says. So we've always had a conflict there, because he is not going to get better. But this year, she sat me down and said, "I understand what you're going through and whatever you have to do, even if you have to put him in a nursing home, I'm behind you."

I have actually thought of putting Cory in a nursing home, but I dismissed the idea because it's not where I am right now. I'm the person who has taken care of him for so many years, and I'm the only one who can make the decision. I've brought up the subject with him, and we've discussed it. He's the type of person who will go along with anything I say. If I got to the point that I had to put him in a nursing home, he would not fight me. But I don't feel there's a nursing home out there that can take care of him like he should be taken care of. I've seen and heard different stories about nursing homes, most of which are designed for elderly people. It would be difficult for someone who's 39 years old, who can't speak for himself, to be understood and to get the proper care. I guess my decision is difficult to understand for someone who is not in the same position I am in.

Yes, at times I have wished Cory was dead. Not because I feel anything negative about him, but because he has a horrible disease that will never end. It's not like cancer, which often is horrible but usually lasts only a few years and then you die. MS patients go through different steps in their lives as the disease gets worse and worse. And you grieve with your spouse as he crosses each threshold to something more demeaning and life-robbing.

About eight years ago, we started getting a home health aide to assist me. I was working a full-time job in addition to taking care of the kids and Cory. It just reached the point where I realized I couldn't do everything myself. Originally, the aide came in a couple of hours twice a week, but then we had to increase the time and the number of days. Now we have someone in five days a week, 9:00 a.m. to 1:00 p.m. Since I work as a bookkeeper with my office at home, I am able to take care of him after the aide leaves.

At one point, I was paying out of pocket $270 a week for the aide. Last year, I talked to the VA and found out they had a respite care program for people like Cory. They told me he could go into the VA hospital for two weeks and it would not cost us a penny. Respite care is to give the caregivers a break. The VA also agreed to pay the full cost of the home health aide. We have had problems finding a good aide, someone who is not only skilled but who is also caring. It was more difficult when I hired the people myself than it is now, since the aides come through a VA-approved agency.

I make sure I exercise and do everything necessary to maintain my health. The worst thing that can happen is for the primary caregiver to get sick. What would Cory do then? Sometimes I wonder how I cope with everything. Of all the things I do for Cory, the one thing that bothers me most is feeding him. Sometimes my kids help me do this. But I can't let them do the other things, like catheterize their father.

I am currently attending a community college to complete my degree. I've always been very independent. I'm not very sociable; I'm the type of person who can have lunch by myself in a restaurant and not care that there is no one to talk to. Oh sure, sometimes even I long to talk to someone, to another normal adult. I've had one friend, a male friend. I worked with him, doing the bookkeeping for his organization. We've gone out dancing or to dinner, just to talk. He wanted much more, and he couldn't understand that all I wanted was his company. Cory never knew I was going out with him.

My life today is not great, and of course I want more from it. But I've come this far, through some trying circumstances and I'm not about to quit now. Some people think about committing suicide to escape, but I would never do that. There's got to be something better ahead for me.

Children: They Also Care

Edward, as well as Marissa's two sons, had differing reactions to their parent's illness. As an older child of a single mother, Edward was forced into the caregiver role, which he accepted with grace and maturity. Roger too accepted his father's disease by adapting to the changes. Randy became angry at first, and then learned to deal with his problems through therapy. The effects of a parent's MS on a child are as varied as the children themselves.

During one of my wife Carole's numerous hospital stays, I told her nurse the story of Edward, the sole caregiver for his mother. The nurse told me that while a teenager she too had been the sole caregiver for her mother, and that as an adult she resented what she had gone through and she resented her mother as well.

But this adult reaction to what happened in childhood does not have to occur, according to Rosalind C. Kalb, Ph.D., a clinical psychologist at the MS Care Center, St. Agnes Hospital, White Plains, New York. Dr. Kalb is an expert regarding relationships between children and parents who have MS. Sole caregiving by a youngster "can be very stressful for all concerned," she says. "It is particularly difficult for an adolescent who is learning to be independent and to separate from the family. Counseling or family therapy is critical for the child and the parent.

"One of the overall things we've seen is that children are affected by the emotional climate in a household and by the mood of the parent with MS as well as by the physical problems," says Dr. Kalb, "but many families more easily accommodate to the physical changes than to the mood swings and emotional reactions."

Resentment can build up in a child whose parent has MS. "It does happen sometimes or sporadically," says Dr. Kalb. "It depends in part on how the disability affects the child's life. A growing child needs time and space to pursue his or her own activities and interests. The MS shouldn't be allowed to use up all of the family's emotional, financial or physical resources."

A child who has never known his parent **not** being in a wheelchair may be more accepting, but the child's reaction will depend on "how the parent feels about being in a wheelchair and how well the parent is reacting to it. The wheelchair is only one part of the entire situation," adds Dr. Kalb.

She emphasizes that children should not be kept in the dark about the disease, but how much a child should be told depends on his or her age. "My basic philosophy is that family secrets don't work and a child's imagination is much more frightening than reality. Kids should know what's going on; they shouldn't have to guess. They want to know that parents are handling the situation and that they will continue to take care of them. Kids also need to be reassured that the parent is not going to die.

"Don't force information down a child's throat. Make information available to them, keeping in mind that every child learns in a different way. Don't expect a kid to read a book about (the disease) and then to have a long discussion."

Learning about MS for a child is a little bit like sex education, Dr. Kalb notes, adding that "you've got to be prepared to answer the questions when they come up" and dole out the information at whatever pace the child can absorb it. "Once children are reassured and know what's going on, they pretty much go about their business."

Sometimes, you have to be somewhat of a psychologist yourself, trying to interpret what your child is really saying. I recall my daughter, Lynn, a teenager at the time, remarking to Carole, "I wish you could go shopping with me like my friends' mothers do."

Dr. Kalb says that "children tend not to verbalize their feelings, questions, and concerns, leading parents to mistakenly conclude MS is not a significant issue in their lives."

And she adds, "Children ... need reassurance that they are not the problem." [1]

Some children also fear they may inherit the disease. Younger children might even fear they can catch MS, like they do a cold or the measles. The incidence of inheritance is, of course, extremely small. Even in the cases of identical twins, where one has the disease and the other doesn't, the incidence of MS being inherited by their offspring remains exceedingly low, although it is 15 to 20 times greater than in the rest of the population, according to studies. But still the risk is only three to five percent. "Many other things in life are more likely to be a problem," adds Dr. Kalb, citing the risk of being injured in an automobile accident or developing cancer.

The bottom line, she says, is that many parents with MS feel that their children "have become more caring, sensitive, and tolerant of individual differences than children who have not had experience with chronic illness or disability."

---

[1] "When a Child's Parent Has MS" by Rosalind C. Kalb, Ph.D., *MS Quarterly Report*, June 1995, published by Demos Vermande, New York, N.Y.

Alan Revisited

In October 1994 I had an appointment with my internist, Dr. Martin Shargel, for my annual physical. In the course of our discussion, he asked me if Carole had tried taking bee stings to alleviate symptoms of her MS. I told him we had read a story in the *Washington Post* about someone in our area who had used bee sting therapy effectively on some MS patients. But I also told him I thought we had gone through enough "cures," from Carole having the silver fillings in her mouth replaced to acupuncture. Nothing had helped.

"I'm normally a skeptic about these things too," he said, "but I've seen it work in two instances, on a colleague's patient, and on one of mine. My patient is a 35-year-old former window washer who was diagnosed with MS several years ago. When I met him, he was flat on his back in the nursing home where I am one of the doctors on call. He could not even sit up in a wheelchair or feed himself. He was also incontinent.

"A few months after I first saw him, he started on bee sting therapy. Within a short time, I noticed a difference in him. He could sit up in his wheelchair, he could feed himself, and he was no longer incontinent."

Amber Rose is a licensed acupuncturist who became interested in how bees could relieve symptoms of various illnesses. She works out of her home, which fortunately is only a few miles from where we live. Carole and I made an appointment and went to see her. We learned that some people with arthritis, for example, have been subjecting themselves to bee stings for years. In fact, apitherapy—the medicinal use of products of the honeybee's hive—is an ancient practice. As someone asked us, "Have you ever seen a sick bee keeper?" Of course I don't count many bee keepers among my circle of acquaintances, but the question is, nevertheless, an intriguing one. We have since learned that most traditional medical practitioners do not believe in the ameliorative effects of bee stings; this type of therapy is, in fact, quite controversial.

When someone opts for bee sting therapy, the person must first be tested to make sure he or she is not allergic. Amber ices the site, holds a bee in a tweezers and places it on the person's body. The sting is immediate; Carole says it hurts but really no more than an acupuncture needle prick. After the sting, you wait about 15 minutes to determine if the recipient has an allergic reaction. Carole did not, although after each of her first few sessions, the stung sites were excruciatingly itchy for several days. A couple of times the itching made her so uncomfortable she considered quitting the therapy. However, after several weeks, the itching was no longer a problem.

Carole went twice a week to Amber's house where she received about 20 stings at a sitting. The bees were placed on various parts of her body, above her pubic area, on her legs, on her arms, and sometimes elsewhere where there seemed to be a need to ease pain or stiffness. For instance, at one point, Carole had a stiff back. Amber placed a couple of bees on her back, and within a few hours the stiffness had lessened considerably.

After more than six months of this therapy, Carole's mental and emotional problems eased measurably. For the first time in several years, for example, she is able to read and comprehend what she has read. Her moodiness and extensive periods of depression lessened dramatically, and she now has more of a positive outlook on life. Physically, she has more strength and is able to lift her bad leg slightly, whereas before she just dragged it.

After about a year, we noticed that the improvement had leveled off. There were no more dramatic changes. Although she was fearful about stopping the stings since she didn't know if the healing benefits already achieved would be reversed, Carole decided to take a hiatus to see what occurred. To date, she has not lost any of the gains she made. While the therapy may not have had the dramatic results for Carole that it had for some others, the improvements we have been able to measure made it worthwhile.

The cost of the bee sting therapy was minimal. At first Amber relied on an individual's generosity. Carole donated $10 a week for two sessions. For a few months we had to pay an additional $7 a week to cover the cost of bees which Amber purchased to replace hives she lost during cold winter weather.

A few months after Carole started taking the stings, I accompanied her, and we both met the patient my internist told me about. The gentleman proudly told us he was ready to leave the nursing home to return to his own apartment, something which once had been only a dream.

Bee sting therapy is only one of many traditional and non-traditional alternatives available to MS patients. "I encourage patients to try these things if I believe no harm will come from them," Carole's neurologist, Dr. Martin Rusinowitz, told me.

Many medical practitioners are concerned about alternative therapies, often saying that gains a patient sees may be no more than normal remission of the disease. "There have to be studies (to determine if some of these therapies help), but you need a large population from the MS community to do it," Dr. Rusinowitz said.

"The tendency of MS to remit, or improve spontaneously, makes it very difficult for scientists and patients to evaluate various treatments," say Dr. Louis J. Rosner and Shelley Ross in their book, "Multiple Sclerosis" (Prentice Hall Press, New York 1987). "In fact, this characteristic of MS has led to many ineffective, even bizarre treatments, not to mention a host of false claims for a cure."

Some therapies are apparently more beneficial than others. And some, such as chelation, which removes excess amounts of metal and minerals from the body, receive a thumbs down from many physicians, including Carole's neurologist, who says, "It could cause harm to the patient."

Here are some of the alternative treatments available:

- **Steroids and other drugs which reduce inflammation**. Carole and many other MS patients have at one time or another taken ACTH (adrenocorticotrophic hormone). In several instances, Carole was helped considerably by the drug, but only for a relatively short time (up to several weeks). The last two times she took the drug, she had adverse reactions to it. One promising drug for people with relatively mild MS is **copolymer-I**. It is still being tested. **Beta interferon**, which only came on the market a few years ago, has been shown in some cases to reduce exacerbations in relapsing-remitting patients. **Cytoxan**, an anti-cancer agent, is also showing some promise, but the National Institutes of Health states, "People who have chronic-progressive MS, the more severe form of the illness, are much more difficult to treat. Drugs for this illness tend to be stronger immunosuppressive agents and carry more serious side effects. Neurologists debate whether these drugs should be used at all."
- **Plasmapheresis**, a very expensive treatment which insurance companies tend to consider experimental and therefore do not cover, involves "washing the blood." The patient's blood is removed and the liquid plasma is separated from the blood cells in a centrifuge. Then the plasma, which contains lymphocytes and antibodies, is discarded and replaced by normal plasma. The reconstituted blood is then pumped

back into the patient's bloodstream. The cycle is repeated several times.[1]

- **Total lymphoid radiation**. This treatment, according to NIH, involves radiation of the immune system, and has been successfully used for 20 years in treating early stages of Hodgkin's disease. Preliminary studies suggest the treatment may help stabilize people with chronic-progressive MS for three to four years. A larger clinical trial is planned.
- **Diets**. Over the years, all sorts of diets have been prescribed for MS sufferers. Dr. Catherine W. Britell, writing on the Internet (address http://weber.u.washington.edu/~britell/), says a nutritious, low-fat diet should be followed. "Although there have been claims that an extremely low-fat diet slows decline in neuromuscular function in MS, scientific data does [*sic*] not support this." In any event, a low-fat diet is good nutrition "for everyone from the standpoint of control of fats in the blood and weight control."

  Dr. Rosner and Shelley Ross in their book say that a 17-year study of MS patients proved that a low-fat diet had no effect on the course of the disease. However, Dr. Britell says she is very concerned about weight gain in MS patients since excess weight can limit mobility and affect self-esteem.
- **Physical therapy**. Dr. Britell says that exercise, done properly, is an effective treatment for MS. When Carole was diagnosed with the disease, her neurologist told her that physical therapy would not help. In subsequent years, other neurologists recommended it, and it was part of the intensive regime she underwent during two separate stays at the National Rehabilitation Hospital in Washington, D.C. From what we have seen, each time she has taken physical therapy, she has improved. Now she does daily exercises, which her home health aide or I assist with.

  A variation on the physical therapy theme is aquatic exercise. It is often recommended because the buoyancy (weightlessness) which occurs in water helps someone with weakened extremities attain greater range of motion. Also, water helps to dissipate body heat generated by exercise. This is important to MS patients who often suffer a temporary worsening of symptoms if they become overheated.

---

[1] "Living with MS—A Handbook for Families," by Dr. Robert Shuman and Dr. Janice Schwartz, Collier Books/MacMillan Publishing Co., New York 1994.

- **Hypnosis**. At one time Carole learned self-hypnosis, and for a while this helped too. "Hypnotherapy takes advantage of the mind/body connection by encouraging patients to enter a trance, a state of heightened suggestabilty," says Dr. Andrew Weil in his book, "Spontaneous Healing" (Alfred A. Knopf, New York 1995). "In this state, verbal suggestions are often able to pass from the mind to the nervous system, influencing the body in ways that seem impossible in ordinary states of awareness."
- **Naturopathy**. Dr. Weil discusses this treatment which comes from the old tradition of European health spas with their emphasis on hydrotherapy, massage, nutrition and herbs. Naturopaths adhere "to a general philosophy of taking advantage of the body's natural healing capacity and avoiding the drugs and surgery of conventional medicine." Some naturopaths use body work, acupuncture, practice herbalism or homeopathy, and they are licensed in only a few states, mostly in the West. Carole has had acupuncture on two different occasions for extended periods, but both times the procedure was of little benefit to her. However, other patients have reported that acupuncture has helped ease symptoms such as pain, spasms or bladder dysfunction.
- **Other treatments**. Chiropractic can provide temporary help for some but, says Dr. Weil, it is less effective with chronic pain syndromes. Biofeedback uses audio tapes and electronic sensors to teach relaxation. Then there is traditional Chinese medicine; Ayurvedic medicine; replacement of silver dental fillings with gold or plastic (which cost us $2,000); hyperbaric oxygen chamber; cobra venom; and even marijuana.

"The surest sign that there is no cure for multiple sclerosis at the present time is the long list of available treatments currently in use. Many drugs claimed to be of value in the past have been thrown out, while others are undergoing study for the future in centers dedicated to clinical trials of new drugs."[2]

All of us who live with this disease, whether as patients or as caregivers, recognize that there is no cure. However, knowledge and action are empowering and for many of us, it is better to light a candle than to curse the darkness.

[2] *Ibid*, p.186.

Jim

I found out by accident that my wife, Judy, had multiple sclerosis. We were separated at the time, and shortly after learning about her illness, we got back together. People have asked me many times if, knowing what I know now, would I have gone back with her? I honestly don't have an answer. I do know I've always loved Judy.

We've been married 13 years now, but it was back in 1988 that she was diagnosed with MS. The first signs of the illness began a year before the diagnosis. She would get extremely tired and she kept losing her balance. We went to the hospital emergency room a number of times, trying to find out what was causing her symptoms, but the doctors couldn't give us an answer.

We're members of a health maintenance organization, so we went to the doctor at the HMO, and he started doing all kinds of tests. At first, he thought the tiredness and the falling were stress related. But the symptoms continued. Then Judy started having vision problems; things were not too clear when she looked through her right eye. Her left eye was okay. When she began to have trouble walking, her doctor recommended an MRI.

Her symptoms started causing a lot of problems between us. The illness made her irritable, and we argued often. I've been a heavy drinker for many years. In fact, I come from a family of heavy drinkers, and I believe I may be a borderline alcoholic. Sometimes I will get blind drunk (go on a bender) for a few days; then I won't drink anything for a week or a month. I like alcohol of any kind, but I don't think I'm so bad that I need treatment. It's something that's in my family, and we all accept it and laugh about it. In fact, in the past few years I've cut it back quite a bit. But my drinking did lead to frequent hassles between Judy and me.

She had her MRI in the morning; that afternoon, while I was at work, she moved out of our house. I didn't find out for a couple of months that the screening test had confirmed she had MS. She had continued on my health insurance plan, and one of the letters came to the house. I opened it and learned she had been diagnosed with the disease. At the same time, her brother was getting married. He and I had been friends before Judy and I were married and we continued to be friends even after we separated. He invited me to the wedding, and of course, Judy was at the wedding too. We started talking and began to date again soon after that. About three months later, she moved back in with me.

We have three sons, ranging in age from seven to eleven. Initially, she had been taking care of them while we were separated, but when I found out she was diagnosed with MS, I brought the kids back home with me.

When Judy and I got back together, I had no idea we would end up in the situation we're in now. She was still able to walk then, although she had started using a cane which she continued to use for about a year. She progressed to a walker, and then one Sunday, coming home from church, she couldn't use the walker to get from the car to the house. I had to carry her. That's when she started using a wheelchair. For the first year, she went back and forth from the walker to the wheelchair, but for the past two years she has been using the wheelchair exclusively. She can't walk at all, and she can't stand very well. In fact, we have to dress her by rolling her from one side of the bed to the other while we put clothing on her. Either the home health aide or I dress her each day. She also has the shakes and her legs and arms are spastic.

The disease has affected Judy's mind. She's deeply religious and is very involved with the church. She constantly tells me she's a walking miracle, that she's going to get better and be fully restored. She keeps herself going by believing that. But at times, I catch her crying and ask her what's wrong and she replies, "Oh, nothing."

We have a home health aide who comes in eight hours a day from nine to five and prepares her meals, makes sure she gets dressed, does her laundry and a little light housecleaning. Judy is incontinent and loses control of her bowels at times. At night, I catheterize her before she goes to bed and then again before I leave for work in the morning. When I travel, the aide who comes in during the day catheterizes her, doing it first thing in the morning and again just before she leaves in the afternoon. Learning to catheterize was not something I would recommend to anyone, but it had to be done, and I was the only one available to do it.

Cleaning up Judy's bowel movements was a bit more difficult to get used to. An adult's bowel movements are quite different in substance and size from a child's. I used to diaper my three sons when they were babies, but cleaning up my wife is quite different. I know it is demeaning for her, and my heart goes out to her. And for anyone who has to do it, it certainly gets in the way of any romantic notions you have about your spouse.

When Judy's condition got very bad, I was really low emotionally. I kept asking myself, "What's going on here?" It got to the point that I completely stopped being the person I am. In our marriage, travel was a big part of our lives. We traveled together and we traveled separately, so we were constantly on the go, doing things either by car or airplane. That has been totally over for the past three years. But about two years ago, I decided to pick up my travel because I wanted to get back to being me. I knew if I couldn't be happy with what I'm doing and who I am, I couldn't be happy with Judy. Most of the travel I do is for business but some of it is pleasure too. My nine-year-old son had a one-week trip with his school class to Paris, so I was able to go as a chaperon. We had a great time.

I've learned to cook, and I must say I'm quite good at it. Even the boys say they like my cooking, and sometimes they quietly tell me I cook better than their mother did. Necessity becomes the mother of invention, the old saying goes, and while learning to cook grew from necessity, I discovered after a while I really enjoyed doing it.

One of the most important things I miss in our marriage since Judy came down with MS is our being physically close with each other. We had a great sex life, an inventive and a satisfying one. Sex was the one thing that probably kept us together before our separation. After we got back together, our sex life resumed but there were problems. Judy was often tired, she had increasing difficulty with positions, she was constantly in pain during intercourse, and finally I found it difficult to penetrate her. A few years ago, we gave up and sex between us just ended. But I still had, and have, physical needs. I resorted to masturbation, and to be honest, this has now become part of my life. I masturbate about twice a week.

I've also had a couple of affairs. You get lonely. You're sitting in a bar somewhere and someone is there and you start a conversation and the next thing you know you're in bed together. Or you meet someone at work and you start a conversation and if things go well you become lovers. I've experienced both of those situations. One affair lasted about three months before we both decided it wasn't good for either one of us. She was a divorcee and she wanted something more. She wanted commitment, and I couldn't give her that.

I don't know if Judy suspects I've been with other women. But I think she must feel I'm doing something. After all, I'm still a relatively young man. At 43 I'm not ready to become celibate.

There has been another aspect to my affairs. I wanted the companionship of a woman, and this need was as important to me as going to bed. It was wonderful to hold a woman's hand, to dance with her, to walk with her, to talk about all kinds of things. It's very difficult to have conversations with my wife about almost anything because of the MS. Following her train of thought, picking the right words, trying not to get into an argument—these are the things I have to be wary of. We had gone for marriage counseling for about a year before we separated, just to try to talk through some of the issues. We even talked to some of the people in the church because, a year before she left me, Judy had said she wanted a divorce. But the people in the church told her divorce wasn't God's will for us. She had come from a broken home, and the church people told her she was acting out some of the same things which had gone on between her mother and father. When she finally did leave me, those same people tried to call her and talk to her.

Of course, our breakup affected our three children. They were confused. They asked, "Don't mommy and daddy love each other anymore? Did we do something to make them angry?" MS compounded their confusion. Their school grades, for instance, have gone down to the point where I've had to put each of them in private school so they could get more individualized attention and instruction.

I've talked to each of my sons individually to discuss what is going on. I've tried to make sure they understand what's wrong with their mother, what the disease is doing to her, and that, unfortunately, she is not going to be better tomorrow morning and run down the stairs and fix them breakfast. They ask all kinds of questions and I try to have answers. How long is she going to be sick? Well, we don't know. How does this make you feel toward your mother? Angry, yes, very angry. We can understand that. All of us are angry. Your mother is too. But our anger should not be directed at mom but at her disease, which none of us has any control over. It is just something very unfortunate that has affected someone we all love.

As I said earlier, Judy is optimistic that she will recover. I'm not. We still sleep together even though she wets the bed. The smell of urine is always present. The woman who comes each day to take care of Judy uses Clorox on the bed linens to bleach out the smell, and we do a lot of spraying with Lysol. But I don't give up. I come from a family that doesn't give up. My mother was diagnosed with ovarian cancer nine years ago. She wanted to know about treatments that would help her get better, and she was told the chance of her overcoming the illness was one out of 10. She said, "Great. I'll be the one." She's still going strong today at the age of 72. Her cancer is gone.

My mother is as helpful as she can be with Judy, but she doesn't have much strength. Judy's mother is also 72, and she has her own health problems. There are brothers and sisters, but Judy's relations with them are strained. As for friends, Judy has a lot of them, mostly through the church. She's still in the choir and she goes to Bible study each week. People from the church pick her up by car and take her to church for these activities. I take her to services on Sundays and holidays.

As for me, I try to get a lot of help to cope with my feelings and anxieties about Judy and her illness. I talk with as many people as I can, although I have not gone to a psychologist or a trained therapist. I find the MS support group, where others have similar problems, to be very helpful. It's important for my mental health to share with others what's inside of me, although at times I think people must be bored with hearing all these things. Sometimes I even bore myself. But I find I've got to get things out in the open. If you hold feelings inside you, you feel like you might explode.

Marjorie

After nearly 15 years of marriage, Craig has asked me for a divorce. He thinks it's for the best, especially since he learned that I have been having an affair with another man for about four years. But I love Craig and I don't want to leave.

Craig and I had an office romance. He was going to school at night, carrying a full academic load to complete his master's degree, and working full-time during the day. Because he was burning the candle at both ends, we thought his minor physical problems came from the stress of his tough schedule. Neither of us had any idea it was MS; in fact, if you had asked us at the time, we would not have been able to tell you what MS was.

Specifically, he was tired most of the time. Today he recalls that, as a teenager, when he tried to catch a ball, his hands couldn't follow what his eyes saw. But we were young, very much in love, and we had our whole lives ahead of us. We believed if you worked hard now, you would reap the benefits later. So we got married and spent the summer after the wedding on a tour of Europe. It was wonderful. There were romantic suppers in Paris, lovemaking in London, exotic trips to the Irish countryside. When we returned to the States, Craig signed up to study for a second graduate degree. We laughed when we said he would be the most educated person in the computer industry and most certainly in the company we worked for.

Shortly after our return to the rigors of school and work, Craig discovered he had little strength in his hands. Eventually he lost control completely. He couldn't hold onto anything. Nobody could figure out what was wrong. His doctors thought it was a neurological problem which some physical therapy could alleviate. Well, they were right. A month after he started physical therapy, he regained use of his hands. But then he started losing vision in one eye. Even today that one eye has never been the same; he still does not have 20/20 vision in it. Soon after the original attack he had to start wearing glasses, but we thought wearing glasses was no big deal, especially when you are studying and working as hard as Craig was. Millions of people wear glasses.

The loss of vision was a clue to Craig's doctors that something was amiss, and that perhaps the vision problem and the hand problem were connected. His internist pinpointed it immediately. He sent him to the hospital to have dozens of tests, tests which caused us concern and raised our stress and anxiety levels. One of the tests involved putting dye in Craig's veins to look for dark sites, or plaques. The test was very painful, and as a result Craig had difficulty standing.

Craig is not an extrovert and he doesn't talk much about his feelings, but after the tests were over and the doctor gave him the diagnosis of MS, he came into my office. He sat down, and for the first time I could remember, he cried. I didn't know how to react. I was shocked, not only that Craig was crying, but I also didn't know what MS was. I certainly didn't have any idea what it was going to mean to our lives later on. We took a long walk and we talked. We were very much in love and very supportive of each other then. We had the attitude that we're going to deal with this like we deal with everything else. We can conquer all; we're winners.

We had been married about two years when we got the diagnosis. Craig was 26 at the time; he's 38 now. Since then, two members of his family have also been diagnosed with the disease. His sister was diagnosed just recently at age 43; a first cousin was diagnosed earlier. Interestingly, we have learned that MS is not supposed to be inherited. Yet, we know of a few other MS patients with relatives who have been diagnosed with the disease.

In the early stages of Craig's illness, the doctors thought his condition was relapsing-remitting because his symptoms would appear and then disappear. He lost the use of his hands but that came back. He had a great deal of difficulty with one eye but most of his sight returned. At one point, his hands were so bad he couldn't hold a pencil or dress himself. I had to dress him. I didn't resent dressing him because I wanted to be a supportive wife. I adored him and I wanted to help him. I thought the situation would only be temporary. Feeding him didn't bother me either. I'm a nurturing kind of person, and we kind of made a joke of it. So I fed him and dressed him for three weeks, and then the strength in his hands returned, and he was able to do these things for himself again.

Before long Craig had a crisis with his urination. It wasn't too severe and he could monitor what he drank to control the mild incontinence. But this became a crucial event, not because of what happened to him physically but because of what happened to our relationship as we continued to live with MS.

Here was Craig, a full-time student who also had a full-time job, and now he had the additional baggage of a chronic disease. Craig was always a loving man and he was relatively supportive. But now he became completely centered on himself. He didn't have his degree yet, he had to keep up his strength to study and work, and then he had to deal with the constant barrage of testing they do for MS. He started to become a very short-tempered, moody person. Oh, yes, he had been short-tempered and moody before. But it was something I could live with. The disease, however, accentuated these negatives; they became more pronounced and more frequent.

Craig began to have sexual problems; he could not maintain an erection during intercourse. This and everything else drove us farther apart, and we began to lead separate lives. Craig was so focused on just getting through each day, and I was working full time also. Eventually we were spending very little time together. The whole relationship disintegrated, although our love was always there.

Communication went first. Then his sexual problems caused all kinds of resentment for both of us. He didn't feel I was understanding enough, and I didn't feel he was interested enough in my needs. We loved each other, yet there was a barrier we could not get through. That barrier was all the junk we were carrying because of MS. Of course we could have said, "Look, we can't get rid of MS, right? So let's chuck the stuff that's causing us all the extra stress (like his degree or my job) and concentrate on us." Instead we just dived deeper into our work.

Then Craig went through the most degrading, painful, discouraging test a man could possibly ever have. At first the doctors said his impotence couldn't possibly be related to MS. In our heart of hearts, we knew it had to be related, but we grasped at straws and listened to them. They sent Craig for a test called the "sleep away camp test." He had to sleep overnight at the hospital where they attached electrodes to his penis. Every couple of hours a female technician would come in and examine his erection. She noted how big it was and how hard. She measured it. The test concluded that he could get a nocturnal erection.

"Doctor," Craig said, "I don't have a problem **getting** an erection. The problem is **keeping** it. I can't do anything with it once I get it."

The doctor recommended we both go for counseling, so we went together to see a psychiatrist. We should have seen a therapist for the other problems we were having in our relationship. But the counseling was all related to how we could improve our sex life. By this time, the doctors had a change of heart and admitted that his inability to maintain an erection was due to MS. They gave us all kinds of things to do which worked completely against us. They took every bit of passion we had left and destroyed it.

For example, if he had a sensitivity problem, they suggested we take a condom and cut off the top of it when we engaged in oral sex. This meant the only thing that's really getting a lot of stimulation is the head of the penis, and this was somehow supposed to help us both have an orgasm. In the meantime, even though I knew Craig wanted to do some other things, I had to stop myself from saying, "Oh, God, the doctor says we're not supposed to try something like that yet." It was just the most horrendous and demeaning experience imaginable. The games they had us play wreaked havoc on our emotions.

During all this time, Craig's problems with incontinence increased, and it became apparent that he would have to wear some kind of accessory. He chose what they call a Texas catheter, which is a condom catheter. It's external and thus avoids all the infections he could get if it were inserted into the penis. A bag which holds the urine is attached to his leg. At the time, of course, we had no idea how it would affect his day-to-day life.

Maintaining any kind of normal lifestyle was inconvenient, difficult, time-consuming, and loaded with a myriad of detail. In those days, so far as we knew, you couldn't send away for catheters and other appliances through mail order houses like we can now. There was no clearinghouse to help us, and no one to teach you how to deal with it. There was only one drug store near us that had the things we needed. Everybody in there was being fitted for ostomies and other devices. I would walk in with my handsome young husband and little baby, and I'd see row upon row of canes and all the equipment that deals with getting rid of bodily fluids. I would get horribly depressed.

Our son was conceived through artificial insemination. My desire to have a child created another problem. I wanted to get on with my life; I wanted a child. I didn't want my whole life to be on hold because my husband was getting another degree or because of MS. We had already been married about seven years. All our friends had children and owned their own homes and had their comfortable little suburban lives. We were still burning the candles at both ends.

Eventually I got a scholarship and got my own master's degree. But it wasn't enough. What else did I want? Well, I didn't have a baby, and I wanted that.

I begged for years and years, and finally Craig said, "When you get to be a certain age, we'll do it." By the time I got to that age, we couldn't do it. We tried everything. Our own doctor tried to help us and that turned out to be very humiliating. Here's how it worked: first we would try to have sex. Then I would try to lift my bottom up and keep it up for 30 minutes. When that method didn't work, Craig tried ejaculating into a tube. Then I would rush over to the doctor's office where she put the semen into a syringe and injected it into my vagina. A lot of times I'd have to call the doctor and say, "My husband's in the bathroom working on it now, please stay tuned."

Finally, we went to a clinic where they were able to tell me exactly when I was ovulating. They had already taken sperm samples from Craig and frozen them, so when I ovulated, I went to the clinic and his sperm was injected into me. It worked the very first time! One time and that was it. I became pregnant.

This whole process was very stressful for Craig, and very discouraging. He called the clinic a dozen times to ask if they were sure they had the right name, if the semen was really his, if he was the father of the fetus. At the last moment before my delivery, he was thinking, "Oh, God, what if the kid comes out looking like someone else."

We finally had our little boy, but our relationship had continued to deteriorate throughout the pregnancy. I felt I was getting very little attention, very little affection, very little support. The truth was, he had almost nothing left to give me.

Craig criticized me constantly, so I eventually felt everything I did was wrong. Our relationship suffered from bad timing. We ended up vying for each other's attention, and it never seemed to work out. When I wanted his attention, he wasn't interested, so he created his own inner world to avoid me. He became very critical, short-tempered, moody, and isolated. He had always been a loner and was never the traditional romantic type. But whatever romance we once had now completely disappeared.

All the degradation, the tests, the humiliation, the fear about the future further accentuated Craig's studious, isolated habits. When he finally finished his degree, he took up a solitary hobby to occupy his time. He chose something that would not involve me—stamp collecting. He would spend hours and hours by himself with his stamps.

My mistake throughout our relationship was in not challenging him on the small things. I never complained because I wanted to avoid trouble. Then the anger and frustration would build up in me and I would become irrationally angry about something which on the surface seemed very unimportant. Of course, my anger would not make any sense to him. I'm sure he often thought "I've got a dingbat for a wife." I was on edge all the time. Sometimes I would do something impetuous or crazy just because I was so concerned about disappointing him or starting another argument. I'd want to ask every day, "How are you feeling?" But I didn't want him to feel I was thinking only of his disease. I just practiced a lot of conflict avoidance. Now I wonder why I didn't say "Isn't there something we can do together?" We had a lot more in common than stamp collecting!

At one point, I asked him to go to a marriage counselor with me, but he said no. Instead, he continued going to the psychiatrist who first talked to us about our sexual problems. I did not like this man because I didn't think he was attuned to our real problems. But Craig liked him because the two of them had similar personalities. So Craig told me I should find my own counselor. I did go to a therapist for a while, but I just couldn't work out the logistics of the frequent appointments. Then I got involved in a support group. I thought I was getting the support I needed from that group, but in many ways the group was working at counter purposes to my relationship with Craig because they encouraged me to concentrate on me and making myself whole and fulfilling my needs. Craig and I continued to drift farther and farther apart.

We had gotten jobs in separate companies several years earlier. Now Craig resented all the time I spent at my job. He wanted me to pay more attention to the family and to him and not to take phone calls at night or bring work home. But I felt I had to work hard because I was so insecure about our future. I knew that eventually I would have to be the breadwinner. We had our son in day care, which cost a lot. Craig's company seemed on the verge of going out of business about every three months, so I felt we had very little security there. He was still "in the closet" about having MS. People at work sometimes thought he was drunk because of his difficulty walking and his irregular gait. He brought his job insecurities to me, and I responded by working harder. That didn't improve our relationship.

Craig had to get up often at night to use the bathroom because of the drugs he was taking. He took so many pills I lost track of what they all were for. His sleep and my sleep were being disrupted, and the lack of sleep in Craig's case was making his problems with MS worse. The doctor suggested he might consider taking an antidepressant, which would help him sleep. Craig asked me if I could deal with his taking the antidepressant because it would mean he would sleep through the night and consequently wet the bed we shared. At the time I was in the midst of diapers with my son, so

I said I wouldn't mind. I didn't want to sleep in a separate bed, and I never have been a squeamish person anyway.

He started wearing an adult diaper to bed, and we put down a waterproof sheet for added protection. This change didn't exactly improve our sex life. Intimacy with someone who has MS doesn't happen easily. You don't just roll over and things start. You have to plan. But through it all, Craig displayed a great deal of strength and dignity, so I just kept my mouth shut about my own disappointments because I had so much pride in how he was handling his problems.

Another turnoff to intimacy is that many people with MS have uncontrollable shakes. When Craig started shaking, I would wonder, "Is he enjoying himself? Am I doing something wrong?" The last thing you want to do when you're having sex is to think. You don't want to analyze things; you just want to do it. Thinking about it is like being doused by cold water. Thus, the times we had sex grew farther and farther part.

At the same time I didn't really understand that, in spite of his withdrawal, Craig was almost begging me to be intimate with him, to have sex. He never came out and asked. Instead he might say, "Why don't we go in late to work on Friday?" It took a long time for me to get what he was really saying. Sometimes we'd make plans to be together and then I would have a meeting at the last minute. He would feel rejected, not only because of what was happening to him physically but also because he felt my work was more important to me than he was.

Craig is extremely knowledgeable about his disease; he probably knows more than his doctors. Because he understands how the human body works, he is able to use his will power and to control his environment. He uses a cane to help him walk. He really needs to use two canes or Canadian crutches, but he's reluctant to use anything orthopedic or that makes him look too disabled.

Until recently, the course of his disease has been relatively slow. Then another problem surfaced. Craig's brother was diagnosed with leukemia and Craig had the only perfect bone marrow match for him. The doctors at the hospital where the operation was to be performed had no experience with a donor who had MS, and they warned him they didn't know how the procedure might affect him. He knew he could become a paraplegic, but Craig felt he had no alternative. His brother needed help, and Craig was going to give him a chance to live a normal life.

When he came out of the procedure, he was far worse. The combination of stress over the possible death of his brother, the mental anguish about the procedure, and the pressures on his own physical system started him on a downward spiral. His mobility worsened. The strength in his legs deteriorated. I sometimes wonder how he stands up. He needs to hold on to walls to walk. His hands have lost their strength again; you can barely read his handwriting now.

Even though we were having sexual problems, the thought of having an affair never crossed my mind. The thought of leaving him or not taking care of him never occurred to me either. I had a commitment; I loved him, and I intended to be there. When a man who was strongly attracted to me asked me out, I was at a very vulnerable point. I went without even thinking. It was just one of those spontaneous things.

I really needed comfort from another human being more than I needed sex. I craved emotional support, the hugging and loving. I liked the attention, the affection, which I wasn't getting at home. And yes, I wanted sex, although I didn't know I wanted it until it happened. My lover was married too, but he did not have a very loving relationship with his wife. There was a lot of talking between us, a lot of supporting. We both needed that.

Our affair went on for nearly four years before Craig found out, although I think he had suspected it for a long time. He found a love note among my things and he was devastated. He told me he knew there was something wrong and that I was miserable and unhappy. I wanted to tell him why I needed the affair but I couldn't. I was so full of guilt. I was miserable while the affair was going on, yet I didn't want to stop.

Craig became physically violent. He punched me in the face. He pulled my hair. He threw me on the bed. He called me obscene names. He told me I should rot in hell. He destroyed things in our bedroom. He insisted I get tested for AIDS. He insisted I throw away anything my lover had given me. He told me to put the stuff in a garbage bag and leave it for him to throw out so he could look through it. He wanted to know every detail of our affair. He said if I didn't tell him everything he would find out anyway, and the only way for us to resolve our problem was for me to be completely honest with him.

I was so frightened. I told him everything. He kept me up at night for nearly ten days, alternately questioning me and yelling at me. I didn't eat. I didn't sleep for days. My son asked, "Mommy, why does daddy always make you cry?"

I have not seen my lover since Craig learned about us. I called him on the telephone to explain what happened. He was mortified and offered me whatever support I needed, financial or otherwise.

All of the things Craig demanded, like testing for AIDS, were conditions he set up if he was to stay with me. Even though I met all his conditions, he said he still needed time to think about whether he would actually stay in the marriage. At that point, I suggested again that we go to a marriage counselor. The counselor said she could tell we really loved each other, but we had a whole lot of baggage to deal with, and she wasn't sure we would make it together. She added that we should give things a couple of months before we came back to her.

After that, our relationship got even worse. Our work schedules did not mesh, and by the time I was able to go back to the counselor, Craig had pretty much decided he wasn't going to stay in the marriage. We remained together another eight or nine months and resumed our intimate relationship. It is obvious that Craig still loves me, but he has been so hurt by what I did and by this terrible disease. Life has just beaten up on this guy.

Throughout the period we stayed together after he found out about my affair, I toed the line. I did everything he asked. He called me at work every day, and I had to make time in my day to call him. I did not see my lover anymore. I told Craig where I was at every moment of the day and whom I was with because he was so suspicious. If I went out to lunch, I told him whom I was going with. If I had a meeting, I told him whom I was going to see and gave him the telephone number where he could reach me. I have no idea if he checked up on me or not, although at one time he threatened to get a detective to follow me.

At first Craig made me believe that things were going to work between us, but he changed his mind. I don't know why. I've asked him, but he won't tell me. Perhaps changing his mind is just another result of his disease and the effect it has had on his mind. I can tell there are times he forgets what I say. But he is so determined to prove that his intellectual prowess is beyond reproach. If I even suggest he is forgetful or anything else related to his mental faculties, he would blow his cork.

Even the way he talks has been severely affected by MS. He has always been a very cautious talker, never said anything he didn't mean, never said an extra word. Now he speaks so slowly and his words are so labored, he often doesn't finish his sentences. People are tempted to jump in and finish his sentences, but he's very sensitive about anyone interrupting him.

When he finally asked me for a divorce, even that became confused. We have a legal separation, but he hasn't decided whether we will actually take the final step. I don't have any say in the matter, because he knows I don't want a divorce. He's moved out of the house. We have joint custody of our son. I still wear my wedding ring. I'm not dating. I couldn't, when I really want to get back together with him.

I'm in limbo. My friends think I'm crazy to want him back because I've been so unhappy. Certainly no one, including me, knows what's down the road for him. I believe he's going to be in a wheelchair eventually. And even though he will never get well, I also believe he can have a good quality life for a long time to come because of his personality and his intellect. If he said to me tomorrow, "Let's get back together," I'd do it.

When Your Spouse Is No Longer the Person You Married[1]

As we have seen with Marjorie and Craig, personal relationships often change when one partner has a chronic disease such as multiple sclerosis. In some instances sexual dysfunction, like other MS symptoms, may come and go. This builds up anxieties in both partners and creates additional stresses and strains in a couple's relationship.

Often, simply talking with your partner can ease concerns. Using your creativity to adjust to the changes created by MS can help you maintain a lively, intimate and satisfying relationship. The National Multiple Sclerosis Society suggests that couples work at sharing feelings with each other, communicate honestly, be flexible about sexual expression, seek medical treatment for physical symptoms, and for nonphysical problems consider consulting a psychotherapist or counselor who specializes in sex therapy.

Because of the wife's illness, one couple I know engaged solely in oral sex, which they found quite fulfilling. In another situation, where the man was ill, he proudly stated that he had a wicked tongue and could satisfy his wife by performing cunnilingus. In many situations, however, sexual activity becomes burdensome and eventually all but impossible. Fatigue, incontinence, and the severity of the loved one's disease may preclude intercourse or oral sex. As a result, some well spouses may turn to other means of gratification, including masturbation or having a relationship with someone else, as both Jim and Marjorie did.

---

[1] Mary Lambert, M.S.W., a psychotherapist who lives and practices in New York City, coined this title as far as I know. I want to thank her for allowing me to use it here.

But an intimate relationship is more than sex. It includes companionship, sharing and caring, taking walks together, holding hands, having a spiritual intimacy. "When a person loses his or her life's companion to chronic illness, it creates a terrible loneliness, a great sense of deprivation, and anger," says Mary Lambert, a psychotherapist practicing in New York City. She adds, "The well spouse thinks, 'Why aren't you the way you used to be? Why aren't you there for me?'

"It takes a long time for the well spouse to settle into a routine; you really have to do a somersault in your life. You have to go from a love that meant equality and full sexuality to having someone often fully dependent upon you, and that takes a lot of work. It's really a question of giving up desires you have. You have to give up wishes. You have to give up a comfortable non-thinking way of relating to a very well-thought out way of relating. That is, all the things that came naturally before, you can't do any more."

Mary Lambert brings a rare dimension to her practice of psychotherapy: she was a well spouse. Her husband had been a vigorous, talented man, a passionate cellist, an avid swimmer, and an independent and caring person. Then he had two strokes within 24 hours, the last one leaving him with a paralyzed throat. He could not eat; he had to be fed through a tube.

He spent five years in this condition until one day, while going to the bathroom, he fell and cracked his head against the wall. The accident resulted in a massive hematoma. Following an operation to relieve pressure on the brain from the hematoma, he returned home where he died seven months later.

When a loved one dies after a long-term illness, often there isn't much mourning because you have already mourned when your loved one was alive and was dying slowly. "That's absolutely true," says Mary. "There's often a tremendous relief when the chronically ill person dies. It took almost six months before I could remember what my husband was like before he had the strokes. Still today, when I go to bed at night, I relive the last seven months of his life, and particularly the last three weeks, which were exceptionally horrible because he died at home."

Mary recommends that when a loved one is dying, if at all possible he or she be put into a hospital, a nursing home, or a hospice where there is good medical care.

In her role as a psychotherapist, Mary says when the spouse with whom you live and love is no longer the person you married, "life requires reevaluation. The secure, predictable moments of happiness together become precarious, plans for the future fall by the wayside, and the relationship itself becomes skewed.

"I think there is something that almost heightens the sexual need for the well spouse when you know there is no possibility of getting sexual satisfaction from your partner. You also need to release your tension. Having good sex can be very satisfying. Yes, one looks for companionship in a relationship, but if you can have the sex in addition, it's a necessary part of life."

She says it is important not to feel as if you are oversexed because of these physical desires or thoughts about sex. "We well spouses are probably the most faithful of all people," she adds, "because we take care of our loved ones.

"People who are divorced, of course, can do whatever they want, but those of us who remain married or together in a relationship with a significant other, if we look for a bit of freedom, it always creates some guilt, lots of anxiety. I try to get across to people that they should try to feel as little of that as possible and that there are different ways of loving. You can love your wife or husband and still have an affair. You can love two people at one time. You know, God didn't say that we can only love one person.

"I do think you begin to look at your ill spouse as a child. You can have more parental feelings toward them than you do sexual (feelings). It takes time to develop ease with that. Where there was equality before, now it's a one-way street."

Mary stresses she is not recommending that everyone have an affair. "Some couples are still able to have sex and to have a good relationship, but I think if you've reached a point where you have nothing in common with your spouse anymore, it is not wrong to do so. I'm addressing the many people who are lying in bed, twisting, turning, tossing, saying to themselves, 'I wish there was someone here I could hold. I wish there was someone I could have some intimacy with.'"

She tells a story about how one friend solved his problem. His wife has a chronic illness. He has a lover, whom he takes trips with and sees about three times a week, "but he always sleeps at home, and he has managed to maintain his equilibrium with both women," Mary says. "The lover is satisfied because she finds the man so worthwhile as an individual. I'm not sure this type of arrangement is all that unusual.

"People who are well partners are often more thoughtful people. We have perhaps a broader view of what life is all about, and that translates itself into being more aware of people's needs. If you have a man once a week, twice a week, three times a week, there's a lot in it for you if you know that he's there for you, that he loves you, likes your companionship.

It doesn't even have to be love to be satisfying."

She says that if the ill partner has some ability to engage in sex, the stamina to do it, and the well partner is willing, "then why not? What happens much of the time, I think, is that there's no desire left on the part of both people. I remember at a meeting once a woman got up and said her husband was incontinent and quite immobilized, but he insisted on having sex with her. She said she just wasn't at all interested anymore, and she found it wearing and distasteful. I said that under no circumstances should she allow him to have his way because that's like rape. The minute it becomes distasteful, the minute there is no real desire on the part of one of the partners—the ill one or the well one—there should be no sex. The decision not to have sex has to be respected by each partner."

In Marjorie's case, after Craig found the note from her lover, she admitted to the affair and told Craig all the details. Says Mary, "I never advocate—and this I am absolutely adamant about—that the ill spouse find out. If you're going to have an affair, don't tell your ill partner. Make every excuse. Don't discuss it with your partner, because that tacitly puts you in the position of asking permission. If your ill spouse finds out about the affair, deny it."

One man told me his wife had suggested he go outside the marriage to seek companionship. Another told his wife about his affair, said he intended to continue it, and that this continuance did not mean he was going to leave her. He fully expected to handle her needs for finance, security, and companionship, but he owed something to himself and he was pursuing what he needed periodically with another woman.

"Even if your ill spouse tells you it's okay to take a lover," Mary adds, "say you'll think about it, and never, never tell if you do."

The National Multiple Sclerosis Society says that most spouses do not divorce their ill partners, especially when the parties have been together a long time. However, Debby Allen, the Cleveland, Ohio, based long-term care ombudsman, says her experience shows that when the ill partner is young the well spouse, particularly if it's a man, tends to file for divorce. "What I have seen, even after divorce, is that the husbands seem involved still," maintaining a link with their former wives who are in nursing homes.

Mary, however, says she doesn't know if it's true that more women than men remain faithful to an ill spouse. "If it is true," she explains, "it may be because men have traditionally never seen themselves in the role of caregiver. And, I think men are much more out in the world, even today, and it's much easier for a man to find a woman than for a woman to find a man. I don't think there are too many psychological reasons for it. Maybe men feel a little more entitled because they don't see themselves in the role of a nurse where women often do."

Mary says that sometimes well spouses should consider divorce. "I know of a case where the man would come after his wife with his cane and beat her, and run into her with his wheelchair, so she finally left him. I doubt that was a very good marriage before he got sick, and I think that frequently happens. You know, not all marriages are made in heaven, although we like to think they are. The public often thinks that all sick people are angels. Nonsense. Sick people can be just as menacing and nasty as well people."

As a caregiver you are responsible both for your spouse's well-being and for your own. In order to be a responsible caregiver, you must maintain your own physical, mental and emotional health. Whether your choice is celibacy, divorce, or a relationship outside your marriage, only you can choose what's best for you.

RX: How to Deal with a Diagnosis of MS

Once the diagnosis has been made, you'll experience a sense of enormous relief. After months and perhaps years of mysterious symptoms and uncertainty about what is wrong, you finally know the answer. You can go on from here. However, you should know that not only has your loved one's life been changed forever but so has yours. It's wise to understand what you will have to do and what you should not do as you face the uncertain days and years ahead.

As you've read the preceding chapters, you've shared what "the other victims" have experienced. While each situation is different, there are many similarities. You will have to chart your own journey in response to your own experience. But you do not have to do it alone. Help is out there, people and places where you can go for information, guidance, and support.

If you have a computer and one of the on-line services such as America Online, AT&T, CompuServe, or Prodigy, which gives you access to the Internet, start your research there. You will find substantial information on America Online, keyword Health. On the Internet, you can use Web Crawler or another search engine and the keywords "multiple sclerosis." Many of the 200+ references we found are home pages produced by MS patients and caregivers. You will find articles by medical doctors who specialize in the research and treatment of MS and similar diseases. Useful publications, information about equipment, new research and commentary about a variety of treatments are there for the reading. America Online has subscription information about a newsletter, *Real Living with Multiple Sclerosis*, which contains much useful and interesting information. All this data let you know that others are dealing with the same problems and frustrations you face.

There are different philosophies and approaches to playing the cards life has dealt. You can fold or you can hold on and fight to make life as meaningful as possible for you and your loved one. In any difficult situation, taking action is the single most empowering thing the other victim can do. I asked the members of my MS support group to share the actions which have worked for them. Below you'll find our recommendations to help the other victims and to aid those who are currently facing the changes this horrible disease has made in their lives.

Here are, not necessarily in order of importance, some do's and don'ts to help you deal with today and tomorrow:

Do

Find a good doctor. You really need a compassionate, knowledgeable neurologist. But finding one is often difficult. Most important, you and your ill partner must feel comfortable with the doctor you choose. The doctor should be up front with the patient and with you, letting you know, first of all, that this is a totally unpredictable disease. He or she should guide you to research sources so you can obtain detailed information about the disease. If he just hands you a pamphlet on multiple sclerosis, walk away; he's not going to be much help. One MS support group member said, "A good rule of thumb is that if the doctor does no harm, he's acceptable." For, in reality, physicians are limited in what they can do, other than to recommend courses of action and to monitor progress or lack of it.

As the caregiver, you should develop the habit of keeping notes about your loved one, and reporting what you see and hear to the doctor. Since each case of MS is so different, it is important for a physician to know specifics about what is happening to an individual. Is he or she having bowel and bladder problems? Do tremors come and go? Is lack of energy impacting so that he or she can't work or take care of simple household chores? Have you noticed any disturbing personality changes?

Get support from family, friends, others. Inventory family and friends early in case you need emergency help. Whom can you count on to help if needed? Investigate hiring a caregiver, even for a few hours a day, in an effort not only to help the patient but also to give you some time to yourself. It is important to assist the patient, and it is vital that you stay healthy. As one support member said, echoing the experiences of others, "For many years I never thought to get someone to help me. I just limped along from one year to the next."

If you become ill, there is little you can do to aid your loved one. One caveat if you hire a caregiver: be prepared for challenges and adjustments.

Caregiver agency advertisements sound as if you will be getting highly skilled, caring, and reliable people to take care of your loved one. Reality is quite different. Yes, there are some good caregivers out there but, in truth, many have limited skills and are not very reliable. Many of them function as no more than glorified baby sitters to the patient. Too many times, the well spouse finds that he or she must show caregivers how to do the most routine of chores. Other times you may suddenly have to change your plans because a caregiver has not shown up at the appointed time. Conditions may reach the point where you have to consider long-term nursing care, either at home or in a nursing facility.

Check your insurance. Few families have the economic resources to deal with the overwhelming cost of caring for a severely ill patient. You should immediately inventory your financial situation. Your loved one may be eligible for Social Security Disability Insurance and Medicare even though he or she is under age 65. Many life insurance policies have disability clauses. Bring policies up-to-date and make certain you and your loved one have living wills and that you or someone else in the family has power of attorney for the ill person. If necessary, go to a financial planner for help. These people can be of special assistance if you are considering applying for Medicaid (medical assistance for the indigent) for your loved one. Medical expenses can wipe out what you have saved over the years, so it becomes prudent to protect as much as you can.

Prescription costs can be burdensome. Some insurance policies cover all, most or some of these costs. In a number of cases, you may be able to buy large quantities of medication at a considerable saving. One source for this service is the AARP (American Association of Retired Persons) Pharmacy at 1-800-456-2277.

Do a minimal amount of contingency planning. You will learn fairly quickly that your life is dominated by a series of crises your loved one faces. Many MS patients are fallers and can easily injure themselves. Exacerbations can be sudden and prolonged. In many cases, they tend to last about six weeks before easing up. Life and death situations can suddenly occur. You'll have to deal with them. Don't make decisions unless you have to, but be prepared for the fact that you may have to make quick changes dictated by the patient's medical needs.

If you own a home or live in an apartment, you have to think about the patient's future needs. For example, will your loved one be in an electric cart such as an Amigo or in a wheelchair? Will you need a ramp so the patient can get into and out of the house with relative ease? Do you have to install a stair glide or an elevator in your home if it has two stories or more? What about the bathroom? Do you need an accessible stall shower, rails so the MS patient can get into and out of the shower without danger, a raised toilet? Should you have carpets covering the floors, or will your loved one be better able to maneuver on wood floors? Do kitchen cabinets have to be lowered so the wheelchair-bound patient can reach them? And, finally, should you move? If so, try to find a home or apartment which is already equipped and wheelchair accessible. In the case of a home, a one-story, or ranch style, is best for maneuverability. An apartment should probably be on the ground floor, especially if you need one that does not have carpets covering the floor.

Some moving and equipment costs will be tax deductible as medical expenses. If the patient has Medicare or Medicaid, some of the equipment expenditures will be covered by these plans. In addition, some private health plans will cover part of the costs.

Check for transportation assistance. One of the major problems caregivers face is getting the MS patient to health care practitioners. Many jurisdictions provide transportation assistance at a nominal cost. Check your state and local agencies listed in the telephone directory under "rehabilitation" or "social services."

Learn where you can get medical supplies. As the years and the disease progress, you will need various types of medical supplies to aid the patient, from raised toilet seats to shower benches to catheters to portable potties and diapers. Learn the different sources of supply in your community through recommendation and through the Yellow Pages. You can also borrow or obtain special equipment, such as lifts, walkers, household aids and wheelchairs, through National MS Society chapters or other agencies. Hospitals or university social service and outreach departments can offer assistance.

Do as much as you can together. Adjust your expectations to a different kind of life and different prospects for the future. For instance, you will not be able to do many of the things as a couple or family you once enjoyed and took for granted. In the early stages of the disease, you may still be able to take trips and go out to dinner. But as the illness progresses, these activities may become increasingly difficult. You may have to do them more infrequently, and all your outside activities will involve a great deal of planning

Your horizons will continue to narrow as the disease progresses. For many years, Carole and I traveled, sometimes across the country. But the burden of having to take various medical supplies and equipment and the fact that she tired more and more easily were major factors in our decision to stop taking trips. However, continue outside activities for as long as you can; they're uplifting for the patient, for you, and for your children. They give all of you a feeling of normalcy.

Take care of yourself. Dealing with the impact of the disease on your emotions is difficult but necessary. Take things one day at a time and adapt to the changes affecting your life and the life of your significant other. You need a survival program for yourself, including exercise, an energizing diet, and outside interests. Create a life for yourself outside the sick room, and make your own decisions about how you will live the rest of your life.

You may also find it worthwhile to get emotional support from a psychologist or other trained counselor. Just talking things out with an understanding, trained individual can have a salutary effect. Friends can help as sounding boards for your problems, fears, and wishes. In the early stages of MS, it is not unusual to say nothing about the illness to family members and close friends. You or your significant other may be embarrassed and decide not to "broadcast" the verdict you have received. But talking about the disease with others will help them understand what's happening, and you may well find a great deal of assistance from them.

By all means, join a support group. You'll find emotional support, free advice, and reassurance. You can contact the National Multiple Sclerosis Society at 1-800-FIGHT-MS for the MS support group in your area. Two other organizations which provide information and assistance are the Well Spouse Foundation (WSF) at 1-800-838-0879 and the National Family Caregivers Association (NFCA) at 1-800-896-3650. WSF members have spouses with all types of illnesses, not just MS; while NFCA strives to meet the needs of caregivers, regardless of their relationship to the ill person or the specific illness or disability.

Don't

Don't stop being who you are. Don't let the disease define you. You can't allow the disease to destroy you and others around you, such as your children.

Don't heed all the advice. You'll get a lot of advice, some of it from concerned relatives and friends. They are trying to help, but they don't live with your situation.

Don't believe all medical claims. You will suddenly hear about many so-called cures for MS. As yet, there are no cures for the disease. You'll hear about various drugs which might help. Check with your doctor to learn if he believes new treatments can benefit your loved one; in some cases, such drugs may be better able to help those with minimal symptoms of MS but have no effect on people who have been seriously disabled by the disease.

Don't cave in to pressure and stress. Try to keep things on an even keel. It's not easy to watch someone you love deteriorate physically and mentally before your eyes, knowing there is really little that you can do for them.

Don't try to be superman or superwoman. You can't do everything. Don't be afraid to get help whenever you can. Take needed breaks. Go on a vacation, even if it's only for a few days.

Don't feel guilty. It's not your fault your loved one is sick. If you do feel guilty, take the proverbial "two aspirins" and call your doctor, therapist, clergy person, or a friend in the morning.

The WSF says you are a well spouse when your partner receives a diagnosis of chronic and/or disabling illness; when you feel like a single parent even though you are married; when your financial security is jeopardized because of the costs of illness; when you have trouble maintaining friendships from "a former life" because others are uncomfortable around illness or disability; when you know your partner's condition is unlikely to improve; when you seldom leave the house because you are afraid what might happen; when you are responsible for a partner's life 24 hours a day seven days a week 52 weeks a year; or when your partner is in a nursing home.

The Foundation says all well spouses face the same problems of anger, guilt, fear, isolation, and grief and recommends that the well spouse take seven steps:

Let go of the old life. You can't vanquish the illness and return your life and the life of your loved one to normal.

Try to build a new family life. This life may involve innovation in the home, the work place and the community. An urgent concern for many is maintaining a normal environment for their children.

Arrange for private time. You're staying in the relationship but not to accept for yourself all the limitations of your spouse's illness.

You are an expert, and you can learn from other well spouses. Few outsiders really understand the truth of your life. You can learn by listening to the stories of others in the same situation and learning from their experience.

Ask for help. Develop new ways to approach friends and family for help.

If you can, try to become an advocate for aid from local, state and federal groups and agencies.

Find affirmation in your role with other well spouses. You don't want to be called a saint by the outside world or be told you're braver and stronger than others; you know you're not. Nor do you enjoy the disapproval which sometimes comes your way when you seek a life for yourself. You don't have to explain any of this to other well spouses who are walking with you in your shoes. You will all cry, laugh, understand, and respect each other, and through that you learn to respect yourself for whom you really are.

Be available to other well spouses when they need you. You are wary about approaching the spouses of the newly diagnosed. You know it takes time to move from the emotions of crisis to those of a life that includes chronic illness with no hope of recovery. A well spouse must reach step one (above) alone.

The NFCA offers 10 tips for family caregivers, many of them the same or similar to those advocated by the WSF: take charge of your life; be good to yourself; watch out for signs of depression; accept the offer of help from others; educate yourself about your loved one's condition, for information is empowering; be open to technologies and ideas that promote your loved one's independence; trust your instincts; dream new dreams; stand up for your rights as a caregiver when dealing with public agencies; and seek support from other caregivers.

The National MS Society suggests that the well spouse ask the partner for help. "In most relationships," the Society says in a booklet entitled, *Taking Care—A Guide for Well Partners* (available from the organization's Education Department at 733 Third Ave., New York, N.Y. 10017-3288), "each partner helps the other through crises. And that shouldn't change after a diagnosis of MS. Problems will arise in your life—as they always have—that have nothing to do with MS; problems at work, problems about money, problems with children, friends and relatives, problems about your health. 'Protecting' your partner from problems is like building a wall between the two of you. Continue sharing your problems and your joys. Both of you deserve the warmth and the closeness of an ongoing partnership."

No one chooses to be a caregiver, just as no one chooses to have a chronic illness. My wife Carole, a victim of MS, thinks of herself as a survivor. And while I am "The Other Victim," I am also the other survivor. Like many others, we face the ravages of a terrible disease every day; yet we have made a commitment to make our lives as meaningful as possible.

Sometimes we can do this together; other times we must do it separately. In our own way, each of us needs and deserves a life.

Appendix

APPENDIX A
Resources

Below is a listing of some of the resources available to caregivers. Some of this information is sprinkled throughout this book. Two excellent publications, which list many more resources, are available from the American Association of Retired Persons, 601 E Street N.W., Washington, D.C. 20049. These publications are *Nursing Home Life: A Guide for Residents and Families*, and *Staying at Home: A Guide for Long-term Care and Housing*. Please note also that the blue pages of most telephone directories list federal, state, and local government agencies which can offer assistance. The Yellow Pages also contain helpful listings.

The U.S. Administration on Aging, the National Association of Area Agencies on Aging, and the National Association of State Units on Aging are working on a National Information and Referral Initiative to help link older people and their families to information and resources. For further information, call 1-800-667-1116 between 9:00 a.m. and 11:00 p.m. Eastern time on weekdays.

AMERICAN ASSOCIATION OF RETIRED PERSONS (AARP)
601 E Street, N.W.
Washington, D.C. 20049
202-434-2277
AARP Pharmacy: 1-800-456-2277

AMERICAN HEALTH CARE ASSOCIATION
1201 L Street, N.W.
Washington, D.C. 20005
202-842-4444

AMERICAN OCCUPATIONAL THERAPY ASSOCIATION
4720 Montgomery Lane
P.O. Box 31220
Bethesda, MD 20824-1220
301-652-2682

AMERICAN PSYCHOLOGICAL ASSOCIATION
750 First Street, N.E.
Washington, D.C. 20002-4242
202-336-5500

NATIONAL ASSOCIATION FOR HOME CARE
519 C Street N.E., Stanton Park
Washington, D.C. 20002-5809
202-547-7424

NATIONAL CONSUMERS LEAGUE
815 - 15th Street N.W., Suite 928
Washington, D.C. 20005
202-639-8140

NATIONAL COUNCIL ON THE AGING
Washington, D.C. 20061-5087
202-479-1200

NATIONAL MULTIPLE SCLEROSIS SOCIETY
733 Third Avenue
New York, NY 10017-3288
1-800-FIGHT-MS

NATIONAL FAMILY CAREGIVERS ASSOCIATION
9621 East Bexhill Drive
Kensington, MD 20895-3104
1-800-896-3650

NATIONAL MEALS ON WHEELS FOUNDATION
2675 - 44th Street, S.W., Suite 305
Grand Rapids, MI 49509
1-800-999-6262

U.S. DEPARTMENT OF HEALTH AND HUMAN SERVICES
Health Care Financing Administration
Office of Beneficiary Services
Room 648 EHR, 6325 Security Blvd.
Baltimore, MD 21207-5187
1-800-638-6833

WELL SPOUSE FOUNDATION
610 Lexington Avenue, Room 814
New York, NY 10022
1800-838-0879

Seven Locks Press Current Offerings

Ending the Explosion
Population Policies and Ethics for a Humane Future
By William G. Hollingsworth

Cloth, 0-929765-44-3, $23.95

Paper, 0-929765-42-7, $17.95

"This is a well-researched, uncommonly sensible, deeply caring, desperately needed book. ...unlike others in the population establishment, Hollingworth offers a set of policies with a fighting chance for timely success."

—Donald Mann, President, NPG

Citistates
How Urban America Can Prosper in a Competitive World
by Neal R. Peirce, with Curtis W. Johnson and John Stuart Hall

Cloth, 0-929765-16-8, $24.95

Paper, 0-929765-34-6, $18.95

"Neal Peirce is the best writer on urban affairs in the country."

—Henry Cisneros, Secretary of Housing and Urban Development

National Public Radio
The Cast of Characters
by Mary Collins
Photographs by Jerome Liebling and Murray Bognovitz

Cloth, 0-929765-19-2, $39.95

"...informative, charming, compelling. It tells the story of a special institution and special people."

—Doug Bennet, former NPR President

On Board With the Duke
John Wayne and the Wild Goose
By Captain Bert Minshall, with Clark Sharon

Cloth, 0-929765-13-3, $39.95

John Wayne's yacht, the Wild Goose, provides the backdrop as the ship's Captain chronicles family activities, stories of famous guests and a revealing glimpse of Wayne.

Organizing for Social Change 2nd Edition
A Manual for Activists
by Kim Bobo, Jackie Kendall, Steve Max

Paper, 0-929765-41-9, $19.95

Updated and complete. The manual for grassroots organizers working for social, political and economic change at any level of Government.

ORDER FORM

Title	*Price*	*Qty*	*Total*
Ending the Explosion	CLOTH $23.95		$
	PAPER $17.95		
Citistates	CLOTH $24.95		
	PAPER $18.95		
National Public Radio	CLOTH $39.95		
On Board With the Duke	CLOTH $39.95		
Organizing for Social Change	PAPER $19.95		

(When you order with this form, your order will be shipped freight-free.) **Total $** ________

Method of Payment

❑ Check enclosed (Payable to Seven Locks Press)

❑ Visa ❑ MasterCard

Account # ____________________ Exp.Date ________

Signature ____________________

Send to:

Name ____________________

Address ____________________

____

City ____________________ State ________ Zip ________

SEVEN LOCKS PRESS
P.O. Box 25689
Santa Ana, CA 92799

Phone 800-354-5348
714-545-2526
Fax 714-545-1572